teach® yourself

creative writing

teach
yourself ®

creative writing
dianne doubtfire
new edition revised
by ian burton

To my husband Stanley with all my love

For UK order enquiries: please contact Bookpoint Ltd, 130 Milton Park, Abingdon, Oxon OX14 4SB. Telephone: +44 (0) 1235 827720. Fax: +44 (0) 1235 400454. Lines are open 09.00–18.00, Monday to Saturday, with a 24-hour message answering service. Details about our titles and how to order are available at www.teachyourself.co.uk

For USA order enquiries: please contact McGraw-Hill Customer Services, PO Box 545, Blacklick, OH 43004-0545, USA. Telephone: 1-800-722-4726. Fax: 1-614-755-5645.

For Canada order enquiries: please contact McGraw-Hill Ryerson Ltd, 300 Water St, Whitby, Ontario L1N 9B6, Canada. Telephone: 905 430 5000. Fax: 905 430 5020.

Long renowned as the authoritative source for self-guided learning – with more than 40 million copies sold worldwide – the **teach yourself** series includes over 300 titles in the fields of languages, crafts, hobbies, business, computing and education.

British Library Cataloguing in Publication Data: a catalogue record for this title is available from the British Library.

Library of Congress Catalog Card Number: on file.

First published in UK 1993 by Hodder Education, 338 Euston Road, London, NW1 3BH.

First published in US 1996 by Contemporary Books, a Division of the McGraw-Hill Companies, 1 Prudential Plaza, 130 East Randolph Street, Chicago, IL 60601 USA.

This edition published 2003.

The **teach yourself** name is a registered trade mark of Hodder Headline.

Typeset by Transet Limited, Coventry, England.
Printed in Great Britain for Hodder Education, a division of Hodder Headline, 338 Euston Road, London NW1 3BH, by Cox & Wyman Ltd, Reading, Berkshire.

Hodder Headline's policy is to use papers that are natural, renewable and recyclable products and made from wood grown in sustainable forests. The logging and manufacturing processes are expected to conform to the environmental regulations of the country of origin.

Impression number   10 9 8 7 6 5
Year   2010 2009 2008 2007 2006 2005

33524.

v

contents

Also by Dianne Doubtfire

Novels
Lust for Innocence
Reason for Violence
Kick a Tin Can
The Flesh is Strong
Behind the Screen
The Wrong Face

Novels for Teenagers
Escape on Monday
This Jim
Girl in Cotton Wool
A Girl Called Rosemary
Sky Girl
Girl in a Gondola
Sky Lovers

Non-Fiction
The Craft of Novel Writing
Overcoming Shyness
Getting Along with People

foreword

The life of the professional writer is an enviable one to many people. To some it even possesses an aura of glamour. Seeing one's work in print or on the television screen; mixing with well-known actors and actresses, mingling with admiring readers at lectures and literary luncheons; being – if one is exceptionally fortunate – handsomely rewarded financially as well. But such moments are bought and paid for by the unremitting labour – year in, year out – of getting words on to paper.

The writer spends most of his working life alone. Not for him the thrill of scoring the winning goal before forty thousand fans, nor the excitement of urging chorus and orchestra through the last movement of Beethoven's Ninth. When the laughter and applause break out in the theatre – or the tears are shed – it's the actors and actresses who are up there onstage. The writer is probably elsewhere, probably already sweating over his next work, while consoling himself – if that is his way – with the knowledge that without him none of it would have happened.

Consoling oneself is the part-time occupation of most writers. Consoling oneself that the book wasn't half-bad after all; that there were *some* good reviews; that there's always a next time. Consoling oneself, more than anything, with the knowledge that there is no justice in the writing world: that some lousy writers make fortunes, while many very good ones earn incomes that make unemployment benefit look lavish.

Dianne Doubtfire knows all this: it permeates all the sound, practical advice she offers in her stimulating book. What she *doesn't* offer is a magic formula, a golden short cut to the glittering prizes. There is none. But any beginner who reads and digests what Mrs Doubtfire has to say will acquire a firm foundation on which to build, and save him or herself a lot of needless disappointment and heartache.

In talking to hundreds of aspirants over the years, I have been struck by how many of them were searching for the basic knowledge needed for getting started along the right road to the writing of good work that someone might be interested enough to buy. And I have wondered why no one wrote an up-to-date book in which all that information was presented for easy assimilation.

Here it is now. It is my pleasure to commend it.

Stan Barstow

acknowledgements

First and second editions

The author and publisher are grateful to the following authors, publishers, agents and literary executors for permission to include copyright material: Richard Adams, *Watership Down*: Richard Adams, Rex Collings and David Higham Associates Ltd; H. E. Bates, *The Jacaranda Tree* and Preface to *The Modern Short Story*: The Estate of the late H. E. Bates, Michael Joseph Ltd and Laurence Pollinger Ltd; Ian J. Burton, two *haiku*; Sam Butterfield, *Fly Kite*: Roy Butterfield and *The Guardian*; Wendy Cope, *Tich Miller*: from *Making Cocoa for Kingsley Amis*: Faber & Faber Ltd; Roald Dahl, 'Beware of the Dog' from *Over To You*: Penguin Books Ltd and Murray Pollinger; Dianne Doubtfire, *The Craft of Novel-Writing*: Allison and Busby Ltd; Margaret Drabble, *The Needle's Eye*: Margaret Drabble and Weidenfeld & Nicolson; T. S. Eliot, 'Tradition and the Individual Talent' from *Selected Essays*: Faber & Faber Ltd and Harcourt Brace Jovanovich Inc; John Fowles, *The French Lieutenant's Woman*: Copyright © John Fowles 1969, reprinted by permission of Jonathan Cape Ltd and Anthony Sheil Associates Ltd; Nadine Gordimer, Introduction to *Selected Stories*: Copyright © 1975 by Nadine Gordimer, reprinted by permission of Viking Penguin Inc and Jonathan Cape Ltd; 'A Mad One' from *A Soldier's Embrace*: Copyright © 1980 by Nadine Gordimer, reprinted by permission of Viking Penguin Inc and Jonathan Cape Ltd; John Hersey, *The War Lover*: Copyright © by John Hersey, reprinted by permission of Hamish Hamilton Ltd and Alfred Knopf Inc; Gerard Manley Hopkins, 'Pied Beauty' from *The Poems of Gerard Manley Hopkins*: fourth edition edited by W. H. Gardner and N. H. MacKenzie, published by Oxford University Press for the Society of Jesus; P. D. James, *An Unsuitable Job for a Woman*: Copyright © 1972 P. D. James, reprinted with the permission of Charles Scribner's Sons and Faber and Faber Publishers; Tessa Krailing, *A Dinosaur Called Minerva*: Hippo Books (Scholastic) 1980; Laurie Lee, 'Juniper' in *The Sun My Monument*: Laurie Lee and Chatto and Windus Ltd; C. Day Lewis, 'A Happy View' from *Collected Poems 1954*: The Executors of the Estate of C. Day Lewis, Jonathan Cape Ltd and the Hogarth Press; Ian McEwan, *The Cement Garden*: Ian McEwan, Jonathan Cape Ltd and Simon & Schuster Inc; Iris Murdoch, *Nuns and Soldiers*: Copyright © 1980 Iris Murdoch reprinted by permission of Viking Penguin Inc and Chatto and Windus Ltd; Edna O'Brien, 'The Love Object' from *The Love Object*: Edna O'Brien, Jonathan Cape Ltd, Alfred Knopf Inc and Robert Lescher; Colin Oliver, *haiku*: Shollond Publications; Jill Paton Walsh, a statement made to the author; Sylvia Plath, 'Insomniac' from *Crossing the Water*: Copyright © Ted Hughes 1971, reprinted by permission of Faber & Faber Ltd and Olwyn Hughes; Roy Russell, part of a letter to the author; Vernon Scannell, 'Cold Spell' from *The Winter Man*: Allison & Busby Ltd; Dylan Thomas, 'The force that through the green fuse drives the flower' from *Collected Poems*: Executors of the Estate of Dylan Thomas, J. M. Dent and David Higham Associates Ltd; Alan W. Watts, *The Way of Zen*: Thames & Hudson Ltd and Pantheon Books, a division of Random House Inc; Dorothy Wright, *The Homecoming*; Kit Wright, 'My Version': from *Poems 1974–1983*: Random House UK Ltd; *Writers' Monthly*: Interview with Anne Sexton from *Writers at Work: The Paris Review Interviews* (Fourth Series), edited by George Plimpton: Copyright © 1974, 1976 by The Paris Review, Inc, reprinted by permission of Viking Penguin Inc and Martin Secker & Warburg Ltd.

The author and publishers also acknowledge the use of quotations from BBC Publications; Lewis Carroll; G. K. Chesterton; Joseph Conrad; *Fowler's Modern English Usage*; Christopher Fry; Robert Graves; Aldous Huxley; Samuel Johnson; Nicholas Monsarrat; Pirandello; William Shakespeare; Robert Louis Stevenson; Anton Chekhov; Evelyn Waugh; Thornton Wilder.

The author would also like to extend warm personal thanks to the following, who suggested improvements: Stan Barstow; Dorothy Branco; Ian J. Burton; Ashley Doubtfire; Stanley Doubtfire; Ann Hoffmann; Tessa Krailing; Graham Mort; Susan Newell; Roy Russell; Elizabeth Stevens; Marjorie Tepper; Constance White; Valerie Wilding; the members of the Isle of Wight New Writers' Group.

Kate Cann, quote from an interview with Kate Cann reprinted by kind permission of The Women's Press, 34, Great Sutton Street, London EC1V 0NL from their website www.the-womens-press.com; Wendy Cope, poem, 'The Law of Copyright', reprinted by permission of PFD on behalf of Wendy Cope. Copyright ©: as printed in the original volume; Richard Curtis, extract from *Four Rules and a Suggestion*, reprinted by permission of PFD on behalf of Richard Curtis. This extract is taken from *Four Rules and a Suggestion*, an article which first appeared in the Observer in 1994 and was reprinted in *Four Weddings and a Funeral, The Screenplay*, published by Corgi. Copyright © Richard Curtis 1994; Della Galton, for extracts from *Better Eyes* and *One Step Ahead* by kind permission of the author; David Higham Associates on behalf of the estate of the late Roald Dahl for an extract from *The BFG*; Jonathan Cape Ltd and Penguin Books Ltd. "The Bottler" from *The BFG* by Roald Dahl, illustrations by Quentin Blake. Copyright © 1982 by Roald Dahl. Reprinted by permission of Farrar, Straus and Giroux, LLC. Jill Paton Walsh, extract from an interview published on her website at www.greenbay.co.uk by kind permission of the author; Philip Pullman and *Young Writer* magazine, quote from an interview published on the Young Writer website at www.mystworld.com/youngwriter; Michèle Roberts, 'A Story for Hallowe'en' from *Playing Sardines*: Copyright © Michèle Roberts 2001; Jackie Winter, extract from *The Ugly Baby* by kind permission of the author.

The author and publisher also acknowledge the use of quotations from:

The Fowler's Modern English Usage; *New Shorter Oxford Dictionary* cd rom; Gordon Wells quote from *How to Write Non-Fiction Books*; Alex Hamilton, *Top Hundred Chart of 2000 Paperback Fastsellers* (no direct quote but Alex Hamilton's figures have been analysed further to produce stats regarding the straight novel and the thriller); Transworld Guidelines for Children's Books; BBC *New Writing Initiative*, The Writers' Room; Reference to William Goldman's *Adventures in the Screentrade*; The National Library for Poetry website: www.poetrylibrary.org.uk

The editor wishes to extend warm, personal thanks to Pauline Burton, Stanley Doubtfire and members of the KCA Players of Kinson Community Centre.

introduction

to the first and second editions

Creative writing must surely be one of the most satisfying occupations in the world and, as with everything else, the greater your skill the more enjoyable your work becomes. When studied seriously, as it deserves to be, it is extremely demanding, but the rewards – in pleasure and often in money – are well worth the effort.

You will have your own special reasons for picking up this book. Perhaps you have no wish to see your work in print but want to write only for your own private enjoyment, setting down your thoughts and experiences, revelling in the beauty of words. Whatever your goal may be – fame, money, therapy or the need to express and communicate ideas – it is vital for you to study your craft if you are to make the best use of your time. You will write in your own individual way, developing your own style, but every piece of writing, whether it is a poem, a letter to the local paper or a novel of a hundred thousand words, must have a *shape*. To master the art of construction requires dedication and sustained effort. 'Success,' wrote Evelyn Waugh, 'depends on natural talent developed by hard work.'

I have been writing professionally for nearly 40 years but I still revise a great deal. This page you are reading was rewritten and retyped eight times before I was satisfied that I had expressed myself clearly, saying what I wished to say, no more, no less. An introduction must contain enough to persuade the reader to continue, but not so much that he or she becomes discouraged.

I hope you won't be discouraged. There is endless satisfaction to be gained from putting your ideas on paper as best you can and going on from there to improve what you have written. We may come very close to perfection, sometimes in a flash of inspiration but usually after a lot of hard work; those are the occasions that delight and renew us, enabling us to face the days of trial and error which are also a part of the task.

Even if you are a complete beginner, an idea you jot down today on the back of an old envelope could be the basis for an influential article or even a best-selling novel, but you will need to learn the techniques in order to develop your idea to the best advantage. It is rare for anyone to succeed as a writer without a considerable amount of experience. There can be no set rules, only guidelines, but the novice would do well to follow them until he can break them with wisdom and panache, possibly producing a masterpiece. Whenever I say 'he' I mean, of course, 'he or she'; what a pity it is that the English language, with all its depth and subtlety, has left us without a personal pronoun which includes both sexes!

It is advisable to study this book as a whole. It would have been impossible for me to arrange all the information in watertight compartments even if I had wished to do so; creative writing has so many varied aspects, mingled and inter-related. Characterization, for instance, is as vital to the short story and the play as it is to the novel; planning, construction and good style are always necessary; so is revision.

Whatever your goal, I hope this book will help you to reach it with maximum speed and enormous enjoyment.

Dianne Doubtfire

to the third edition

Dianne's book *Teach Yourself Creative Writing* has always been the next best thing to attending one of her courses. Now it has fallen to me to revise and update the material for this new edition.

I joined her Isle of Wight adult education class in September 1975 and haven't stopped learning (or writing) since. I am one of many former Dianne Doubtfire students who can say, 'joining her writing class changed my life'. An infectious enthusiasm for writing plus her ability to impart complex topics with clarity and ease made her a gifted teacher who has set many a student on the road to success.

I hope you will gain a sense of Dianne the person in these pages as well as benefit from her wisdom along the way.

Ian Burton

part one

getting started

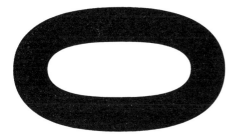

In this chapter you will learn:
- about the three stages in a writer's development
- how to organize your time to write
- what you will need to get started.

Writing for love – and money

This book is designed primarily for the new writer who wishes to see his or her work in print; most beginners feel the need to communicate their ideas and to receive the proper rewards. Those who have no such ambitions, however, will learn to improve their writing and thereby take more pride and pleasure in it.

People sometimes think that there are two kinds of writers, clearly defined and poles apart: those who write for love and those who write for money. There are the sensitive, artistic writers on the one hand, they say, men and women of integrity who would rather die than 'prostitute their art', and on the other hand there are the hard-headed commercial hacks who write for money and money only, and will produce any kind of trash provided there is a big cheque at the end of it. This, of course, is nonsense. It is not only possible but desirable to write for love and money at the same time; the two aims can complement one another.

Exploring and experimenting

The secret of success is twofold: first to discover, by trial and error, the branch of writing which is right for you, and second to master your craft so that you can produce the best you are capable of in your chosen field. To write for love as well as money you must reach a high standard *for your own satisfaction* and not just in order to sell your work. I think it is a grave mistake, even from a financial point of view, to write with only money as your goal; those who write from the heart with dedication and sincerity are far more likely to win fame and fortune. Their writings will endure because the perceptive reader recognizes sincerity and warms to it, remembering the author's name and seeking out his or her works. No one can deny, of course, that there is big money to be made from novels that exploit the undoubted appeal of sex and violence, but first, whatever kind of book you want to write, get down to work and learn your trade. A gifted and experienced writer can handle any theme and stamp it with lasting literary quality.

Needless to say, I profoundly disagree with Samuel Johnson when he pronounces that 'No man but a blockhead ever wrote, except for money'. To prove the fallacy of this – if proof were needed – we have only to think of the millions of children, all over the world, who produce their poems and stories with no thought of payment. Are we to believe that in adult life they suddenly turn into blockheads if they continue to write on impulse for no other reason than their own delight?

What are your chances of success?

This book can present only my personal views, wide open, of course, for discussion and possible disagreement, but the following qualities seem to embrace the essentials for success: talent – sincerity – technique – perseverance. 'But what about luck?' you may ask. 'Doesn't it depend on whether you happen to get your book to a publisher ahead of someone else with a similar idea?' It's certainly true that timing, choice of subject and the personal preferences of people at the top can be propitious or otherwise. But I think you should forget about luck, both good and bad, and simply get on with the all-absorbing task of teaching yourself to write.

How can you tell if you possess the necessary talent? Most potential writers have an instinctive love of words and a gift for stringing them together. Can I hear you saying, 'Yes, that's *me!*'? Then what are you waiting for? People will always delight in a good story, and a regular influx of new writers is constantly in demand, whatever the economic climate.

That said, there is far less fiction published than non-fiction – more than ten times less – so if you are a factual person you have particularly favourable prospects.

Humour, travel writing, lifestyle and how-to-do-it books are ever popular; it's just a matter of using your knowledge and experience to the best advantage. Fiction and non-fiction are of equal importance; it's the quality that counts. So discover and follow your natural bent and don't be tempted to go against the grain.

The three stages

Writing for pleasure

There are three stages in every writer's life. The first is one of blissful ignorance. You write for pleasure, freely expressing yourself, quite satisfied – even delighted – with what you are doing, although it may turn out to be shapeless, wordy and full of irrelevancies. Some people, writing alone without guidance, never advance beyond this stage.

Identifying mistakes and rewriting

The second stage arrives when you join a writers' circle, attend a course on creative writing, or read a book like this. You discover with a pang of dismay that there is a great deal more to this writing game than you ever dreamed of, and that although your work may be 'promising' you have a lot to learn and it won't be easy. You see your mistakes as if they had suddenly appeared in block capitals but you have little or no idea how to put them right. That beautifully sensitive and atmospheric short story you wrote last month isn't a short story at all, you discover, it's a sort of hybrid story-cum-anecdote with no beginning, middle and end – at least, not in that order!

At this stage the novice, torn between the longing to express himself spontaneously and the need to be published, is inclined to fight shy of the whole project. This is quite understandable. He is deeply disappointed to learn that his work is full of faults when he had thought it reasonably accomplished. He feels inadequate, and the fear of failure is hard to dispel. If you are faced with this dilemma, take heart from the certainty that most professional writers have felt exactly the same. I know I did. This is the stage which will determine your future as a writer, so don't give up. I wrote 57 short stories before I had one accepted, and later went on to publish 13 novels and six non-fiction books. If you plan your campaign with confidence and optimism you have every chance of success. I've had students who made such progress that they received cheques for articles and short stories while they were still attending my classes. Of course, it's exceptional to sell your work so soon, but a talented person who is eager to learn, ruthlessly self-critical and prepared for sustained effort can achieve success remarkably quickly. Stage two can last for months or for years, depending on your determination.

Producing the best you are capable of

Stage three brings true satisfaction. Now you can see your faults and you know how to correct them. You understand exactly how to revise your work – pruning, rearranging, discarding, polishing – until you have produced a piece of writing, be it long or short, fiction or non-fiction, which satisfies your newly acquired high standards and will be likely to please an editor. There will always be a gap between the dream you cherish and the best you are capable of, but this is surely a part of the joy – the striving for an elusive perfection, the gradual improvement and the ever-growing sense of power over words. 'They're all there in the dictionary,' someone quipped at me when I was an unsuccessful beginner, 'all you've got to do is sort 'em out.' That was the day I might have given up, but we all have to contend with the pessimists who will try to warn us off or ridicule our enthusiasm. You must disregard them and work with care and confidence towards your goal.

Finding the time to write

'Dividing the day into manageable portions,' said Robert Louis Stevenson, 'brings peace of mind and healthful activity of body.' This is what we must do if we are to succeed in the craft of writing. For anyone with a full-time job – and running a home is one of the most demanding of all – it can never be easy to organize the extra time you need. An hour a day will do to begin with, provided it is *regular*. Later you will almost certainly want to give more time to it and something will have to be curtailed – reading, watching television, gardening, meeting friends. A serious writer, one who is destined for success, is always prepared to make sacrifices. People have often said to me, 'Oh, I know I could write a book if only I had the time!' I nod and say nothing, knowing that the talented and dedicated writer will *make* the time, no matter what the difficulties. After all, if you work for eight hours at some other job and sleep for eight, you still have another eight to play with. Even if you have demanding hobbies, a demanding family, you can surely manage to steal an hour or two for your writing. When my son was small I got up at 4.30 in the morning because that was the only way to find a couple of hours when the house was quiet and I wasn't too tired to concentrate. If you're a late-night person, maybe you could burn a little midnight oil. And if you have been used to sleeping for eight hours, why not give yourself a three-week trial of managing on seven. I never thought it would work for me, but it has.

Avoiding distractions

Most writers feel that it is incredibly difficult to start, even with plenty of time at their disposal. I find myself writing letters that could easily wait, reading the paper (which always depresses me anyway), varnishing my nails, sorting out recipes – *anything* but getting started. And yet, once I begin, I can hardly bear to stop.

My solution is to remind myself that these wasted minutes will never be returned to me and that if I get some work behind me I shall be happy. 'You'll be *miserable,*' I tell myself, 'if you don't get another chapter finished today.' And that's what does it. I don't want to be miserable – especially as a result of my own laziness – and so I begin. I aim to work for six hours every day, but even if I only manage a thousand words in that time (and cross out half of them!) I'm satisfied. I've been working towards the end of the book, and trial and error, as I'm always reminding myself and other people, is part of the task. Make your own deadlines until you have an editor or a publisher to make them for you, and try to practise discipline in fulfilling them. Use the time you have set aside, *even if you appear to have nothing* to *write.* This is the way to learn your craft as speedily as possible.

Tools of the trade

You can manage without a computer or a word-processor for a while, if need be. Even though you may always write your drafts in longhand, as I do, your final draft must be typed/printed when you are submitting it to an editor. It is helpful to 'see it in print' as it were, to get a correct impression of your paragraphing and the general look of the thing. You will find that you can improve your work still further at this stage.

It is impossible for me to work directly on to a machine of any kind; the creative process is strangely blocked. Imagination atrophies. I know many fiction writers, including two Booker Prize winners, who feel as I do, and Joseph Heller, author of *Catch 22,* says, 'I can't write on a typewriter. When I tried to work with a machine I'd do more, but the writing would be terrible. The hard, arduous process of composition I have to do with a pad and a pen.' We all have our individual preferences and I will go into these more in Chapter 21.

What you will need to get started

On your desk, if you have one (or in a drawer or a box if you are working on a table which has to be cleared for meals), you will require the following items:

- ideas book for noting down a brainwave the moment it arrives
- large loose-leaf notepad
- pencils, pencil sharpener and rubber; or a pen if preferred
- paper clips
- A4 typing paper (in America 216 × 279)
- scrap paper

- envelopes
- a cassette-recorder and tapes would be very useful. There is no better way of detecting faults than by reading your manuscript aloud and hearing it played back.

You will also eventually need a reference book or two and you'll find a list of suggestions in the References and resources section of Chapter 22. However, there's something else you'll need long before – an idea.

Getting started

Let's say you have an idea which pleases or intrigues you. You feel ready to write the first sentence. What happens next? Everyone has his own way of working and you will develop the method which suits you best, but here are some suggestions to get you started.

First of all, think about your idea very carefully and ask yourself that vital question: 'What am I trying to *say?*' Whatever branch of writing you attempt, that same question is always relevant.

The next thing is to decide which medium is the most appropriate. Perhaps the short story or a radio play or a poem might be a vehicle for your idea. Sometimes you can only discover the right medium by trial and error. An idea can begin its creative life as a poem but develop into a novel later when your thoughts return to the same idea.

Planning versus spontaneity

By the time you have come to a decision, you may have already scribbled down that opening sentence and beyond. This may be the right time to pause and to prepare some rough notes on the beginning, middle and end. A certain amount of planning is always necessary but some people require more than others. When I ask my students to write down their main writing problems, the same two always head the list: how to start, and how to get shape into your work. They are closely related because the shape must be part of the original plan, even though it may require adjustment – or even radical change – as you go along. The argument against writing a story or an article straight off in a wild rush of enthusiasm is that the lack of planning is pretty sure to be apparent unless you are highly skilled. Thus you will find that you have put unnecessary work into something which could have been improved by more initial thought.

In the next chapter we will explore ideas and how to develop them in greater detail but for now let's concentrate on just one idea – the first exercise in this book.

Exercise 1

Write a short anecdote (300–500 words) with the title 'Seen Through a Window', describing what is seen and the feelings of the person looking. This person may be you or someone imaginary. Similarly, whatever is seen may be real or fictitious. This is a valuable exercise as it gives the student experience in writing about emotions as well as the outside world. The window frame provides a boundary and the writer who keeps within that boundary will learn the vital discipline of restraint. The reader's attention will be concentrated in such a way that he will be looking through that window himself and sharing the feelings of the viewpoint character.

Here are a few examples: a homeless person looking into a luxurious drawing room; a child looking into a doll's house; a fireman on his ladder looking into a burning room; a bed-ridden woman looking out of the window at the garden she used to tend; a man looking in a shop window at something he longs to buy but cannot afford.

My students have always enjoyed this exercise and of course there is no end to the number of times it may be attempted. On many occasions the resulting piece has formed the basis for a short story and has even sparked off a successful novel.

ideas and inspiration

In this chapter you will learn:
- how to keep track of your words
- how to develop your ideas
- the potential of your ideas.

Making your words count – and counting words

At the end of Chapter 1, I suggested the number of words you should aim for in attempting the first creative writing exercise – between 300 and 500. At first sight this may seem to go against the creative grain. What is there to be gained, you may ask, from knowing how many words you've used when all you want to do is forge ahead and explore the idea? There are reasons.

A *rough* estimate of how many words you have used so far will tell you how far you have travelled on that particular journey – approaching the middle perhaps or moving on towards the ending. This awareness will help to give your work *shape*. As you become more practised you will know instinctively where you are in your manuscript. To get a rough estimate all you have to do is to count the total number of words in ten lines and divide to get the average number of words per line. Now multiply the average by the number of lines you've written so far.

Later, if you submit that piece of work to an editor, you should provide a much more accurate word count, rounded up or down to the nearest 50. Magazines and journals work with limited space, the page is finite.

It may help to think of the given length of the exercise as a canvas upon which you are creating your word pictures. No matter how large, the space available is limited. No one would have said to Monet, Van Gogh or Turner, 'Yes, wonderfully expressed, but how much better it would have been if only you'd had a larger canvas to work with!'

If you are using a computer, there will probably be a word count facility providing this information on demand but you should use this feature sparingly while you are writing as it could become a distraction. Where appropriate, the exercises in this book will provide a guideline as to the length your piece should be. Do try to stay within the limits suggested.

Adopt good writing habits early, use words sparingly and always be prepared to edit your work. We will look at the techniques of editing in detail in Chapter 12.

Remember, don't count every word but make every word count.

Developing ideas

'Write what you know' is probably the most quoted piece of advice to new writers. Your experiences, and those of people close to you, provide a rich source of material for both fiction and non-fiction. Your hobbies, your job, the places you have visited, the people you have met will prove to be fertile areas. Once you begin to look for ideas and topics you will soon realize they are all around you.

To demonstrate this, take stock of the things you have done. Draw up a list of the places you have been to, the jobs you have done, the people you have worked with and the things which interest you, including hobbies. Add to your 'list' the interests of your family and the people they have met and their experiences and you will begin to realize what a wealth of material there is to write about.

This 'brainstorming' approach is a useful method to find new ideas and to help break a subject down into topic areas to reveal a specific topic to write about. Your work is more likely to be focussed if it concentrates on a single aspect of a wider topic.

Writing about yourself and your family

There has been an enormous increase in the number of people interested in tracing their family history due in no small measure to the growth of the internet. When the 1901 Census for England and Wales was made available to the internet in January 2002, it received 50 million 'hits' or visits and the site had to close within a few days. Efforts have had to be made to find ways to cope with the level of demand.

A family tree complete with accurate dates, references and relationships is one thing but what about the people? Perhaps your recollection of, say, your grandfather could convey an *impression* of what he was like as a person to those who didn't have the opportunity to meet him. What do you remember most about him? A speech mannerism, favourite sayings, the clothes he wore, the changing weather of his moods. What made him laugh, what made him sad? Writers create word pictures of places and situations but when the process is applied to people it is called characterization, and we will look at this important topic in more detail in Chapter 8.

What a worthwhile task, providing your present and future family with an impression of your immediate (or distant) ancestors, and all drawn from your researches. As your work progresses it may occur to you that you have a series of articles about a particular era which might interest a wider audience, sparking their memories too. A single incident could form the basis of a short, stand alone piece. There are 'nostalgia' magazines packed with contributions from their readership passing on recollections in an entertaining and concise way.

Exercise 2

Write no more than 500 words on a particular relative or person you remember from childhood. You may consider writing a series of these 'character studies' for later development.

Write your best ideas down

Ideas can occur at any time and often at the most inconvenient moments! You may think you could never forget a really good idea but it can so easily happen. Keeping a small notebook handy is a simple solution. In fact, you could find yourself having several dotted about the house, just in case. Don't attempt to write the whole idea down verbatim – develop your own shorthand and try to jot down only key words sufficient to trigger you off again later.

Don't let the new ideas hamper the old ones! If you were already working on something – a short story, an article or a poem perhaps – don't be distracted by the latest idea. Ideas will wait if they have to. They can germinate and grow, become stronger, providing you have planted them, so to speak, on a page (or screen) for later reference!

It is in any case a mistake to start several projects all at once. Aim to finish whatever you begin at least to first draft standard before moving on to tackle the next idea.

Choosing which idea to work on

You might ask, 'But how do I choose which one to work on first?' Most often the idea will choose you. You'll know which is *the* one because it will excite you, perhaps fascinate you so much that you are unable to get it off your mind and that's obviously the one you must give your attention to first. However, the choice is not always so clear cut.

Let's say you now have a list of good ideas and topic areas. Some may seem too difficult and you might be tempted to put these to one side until later when you are 'more experienced'. But if one of these is *the* idea which excites you now, then don't be put off by the difficulties presented, don't delay. It's possible that once you begin to plan the piece, that is to think about the beginning, the middle, and the possible ending, it will start to take shape.

Ask yourself the question posed in Chapter 1: 'What am I trying to say?' and those seemingly impossible difficulties will step back a few paces. Now you can begin the project and deal with those problems later when you need to.

The nature of ideas

Is your idea fiction or non-fiction? Is it long or short? Is it currently no more than a collection of indefinable feelings which seem to have coalesced vaguely, searching for words? In the latter case the idea may find a home in a poem, or even a series of poems within which you try to find those exact and exacting words. Poetry is examined more fully in Chapter 14.

Has your idea blossomed because you realize suddenly that you are an expert in ... what? An item on your ideas list? Something to do with your job or your hobby? Or perhaps you know virtually all there is to know about rearing a dangerously ill kitten who grew up to be a very special cat indeed? You have pictures. You have a rough diary of events and with a bit of effort the details could be pieced back together and the gaps filled in. Is this idea an article, a series of articles, possibly even a book? In the next chapter we will look at how to write an article and later, in Chapter 19, examine the non-fiction book.

What if your idea arrives in the 'ghostly' form of a plot? You might have posed that most rewarding question, 'what would happen if ...'? Even at this early stage your story may already have a vague shape. You know the beginning, there's a super twist at the end and it promises to be a sure-fire magazine short story – then why not write your first draft and turn to Chapter 5 where we will discuss the magazine short story.

Does your idea swirl around a single character, or a set of characters, slipping between them like mist yet somehow linking them all? Silly though it seems, that intangible mist could be the very thing which provides the theme and the conflict and even the plot for a novel. The novel is explored in depth in Chapter 15.

Experimenting with words

Ideas can form just by experimenting with words scribbled on a notepad on the bus or keyed onto a blank computer screen. A word doodle could quickly turn into a poem given the encouragement of your time and attention.

If you have a computer and are connected to the internet you can have a word delivered to you each day by email together with details of its origins, history etc. Visit the Merriam-Webster website at www.merriam-webster.com where you will find details of how to subscribe to the free daily email service. You will also find more wisdom and word games which may give rise to a host of ideas. Today's word? Immutable. We have already seen that no unfinished piece of writing should be immutable, that is, unchangeable. What words rhyme with immutable? – computable, indisputable... there must be more! The fuller definition of the word reads, 'not capable of or susceptible to change'. Have you ever met anyone who could be described as immutable?

If you are new to computers or the internet, Chapter 21 has sections just for you and these may help you to decide whether or not they are your 'thing'.

Exercise 3
Just for fun, set yourself the task of writing an eight-line verse which makes valid use of the word-of-the-day. If you do not have access to the internet choose a word at random from the dictionary and explore its possibilities.

Readers' letters in magazines

Everyday experiences can be fruitful territory for ideas. Many weekly and monthly women's magazines encourage readers to write to their letters pages and most pay very well for those published. An overheard comment in a supermarket might inspire you to write a humorous letter. Getting the 'story' down into the 50 to 100 words average will test your editing skills! If you have children or grandchildren they will probably provide a constant stream of material.

If you have strong opinions on a topic recently dealt with by the magazine you may wish to join the debate – or get one started! These letters are very popular with editors. The key word in this form of writing is brevity, refining a complicated thought into simple words, and it provides great practice. Don't be afraid to draw from your experiences. It's worth remembering that writers seldom invent; they observe, interpret and seek to understand.

Exercise 4

How often have you heard an author being interviewed say, 'I got the idea from a snippet I read in the newspaper. It intrigued me.' Read a newspaper or watch the news on television to see if there's a 'snippet' which sets your imagination in motion. Write no more than an A4 page in note form developing the idea. Experiment with a 100-word opening.

how to write an article

In this chapter you will learn:
- how to choose a subject for an article
- using market research techniques to identify suitable markets
- how to approach an editor.

What *is* an article?

An article is not fiction, although it might contain semi-fictitious anecdotes or imaginary dialogue to illustrate certain points. It is a factual piece, sometimes described as a feature, and usually conveys information (Take your Caravan to India; How to Edit Your Own Videos; Better Health through Autosuggestion; Installing a Garden Water Feature).

If you want to be published, you must avoid the essay-type article which is reminiscent of a school composition, describing a minor personal experience or a private opinion. If the situation is really outstanding it could be a winner, but it is a sad fact that the general reader has little interest in our ordinary activities, however well we describe them. Moving house, holidays that went wrong, opinions on the social ills of the day, etc. are usually non-starters.

Letters to newspapers are the exception; here the new writer stands a good chance of getting his personal views into print if he can express himself in a lively way, with every superfluous word cut out and no deviation from the main point. Excellent practice, in fact, for the potential article-writer.

The best way to learn how to write is to write, so why not begin an article at once? You have only to look at the range of magazines on display in an increasing variety of shops to realize that there is a constant demand for new material. Most magazines buy work from professional freelances although regular features are done by staff writers. Study the list of newspapers and magazines in the current *Writers' and Artists' Yearbook* (published annually by A. & C. Black) or *The Writer's Handbook* (published annually by Macmillan) to find their requirements. You will be encouraged to discover that there are around 650 of them!

Choosing a subject

Successful articles usually fall under one of three headings:

Specialized knowledge
A subject about which the writer has a thorough knowledge (beekeeping; Beijing; teaching deaf children; computer graphics; watercolour painting; vegan cookery).

An unusual angle

This involves taking an ordinary subject and applying a fresh angle to it, for example an article about family meals might be too ordinary but planning them around the World Cup or the Olympics might be interesting (see Topicality below).

Humour

If you can write a really funny – and I mean hilarious – article, almost any subject is suitable (Don't let your wife teach you to drive; The first time I baby-sat; How to gain weight without even trying).

Topicality

If you are still short of ideas at this stage, try a topical theme. This will entail research if you are not already an expert on your chosen subject. You could write something for the centenary of the death of some famous personage, perhaps with local connections, or work out a humorous piece for Hallowe'en. You will find that the more articles you write, the more readily ideas will come to you. When you read a magazine you will say to yourself 'Why didn't I think of that?' Remember to jot your ideas down quickly and once you have learnt the technique of constructing a well-written, entertaining article you may find that you can sell your work quite easily.

Market study

It is essential to study the magazines you wish to write for. This should be self-evident but it is remarkable how often it is overlooked. I know a man who sent an article on karate to a genteel magazine for ladies. 'They should all learn how to defend themselves,' he said.

The magazines you choose for market study will usually be the ones you enjoy reading, the ones that specialize in your particular interests.

What to look for in a magazine

1 Study the length, style and content of every article in several recent issues (editors and policies are frequently changing) and make a note of your findings.
2 Take particular note of the way the magazine presents its articles on the page, that is, the page layout.

3 How many photos are used?

4 Are paragraph headings used to break up the text?

5 Are text or fact boxes used to provide the reader with additional or summarized information outside of the main text, for example, listing useful addresses, sources of further information, etc. If this is so you should take this into account when writing your article, demonstrating to the editor that you are familiar with the style of the magazine in question.

Page layouts and style

Visualize your article on that page. The page layout will affect the way you write the piece because on the published magazine page there will be a headline title and perhaps a 'strap line', that is an intriguing line tempting the reader to read on, along with photographs and/or illustrations. All of this affects your opening line and your opening paragraph because the reader has already taken in a lot of information, so there's no need to reiterate. Instead your feature can start immediately without needing a long introduction to establish the background.

Length

In the course of your market researches you will discover that the length of an article can be anything from 500 to 2000 words or more. A good average is 800. As we saw earlier, a rough estimate of the number of words is all that is needed.

Fillers

Articles of fewer than 500 words are classed as 'fillers' and are used to fill odd spaces at the bottom of the page. The *Writers' and Artists' Yearbook* gives a list of magazines which consider filler paragraphs. Photographs and/or illustrations are not usually needed for fillers except at the discretion of the editor.

Exercise 5

Decide on a subject area – your notes from the previous chapter may help you here. Conduct market research on several magazines as outlined above. Keep separate notes on each title for later reference.

Your first full-length article: a step-by-step guide

1 **Choose your subject** making sure that it falls under one of the three headings listed previously. It must be a theme that really interests you, otherwise you cannot hope to engage your reader. If your subject is too large for a single article, then break it down into topics and then decide which topic area or aspect of the subject you want to write about most.

2 **Select a possible market**, even though you are as yet unpractised. A definite goal will give you an incentive to make a determined effort. Note, professional writers usually decide on a market for their articles and short stories even before they begin to plan them.

3 **Think** out all the possible points you might make in your article, jot them down in any order to form a rough list.

4 **Sort** out the best, discarding any points which are repetitive or not strictly related to the subject.

5 **Decide** whether or not photographs will be needed to illustrate the piece. Decide also whether you need more up-to-date information. The internet will probably be able to help. These days it is often possible to do a lot of your research without leaving home but if all else fails take a notebook to your reference library.

6 **Plan** the order of your points, bearing in mind that the opening must have real impact. It is sometimes a good idea to begin with a question which involves the reader at the outset. The various points you have jotted down must now be arranged in a logical sequence so that the paragraphs flow smoothly towards a strong ending; this means you should save your most vital point till last.

7 **Write the first draft**, improving on your original plan where necessary. When you have written the whole article you will see more clearly how to prune it and rearrange it. Be sure to cut out everything that might be described as 'waffle'. This is the way to streamline your prose and keep the reader's interest.

8 **Choose** a short, snappy title (see Chapter 13, Finding Titles).

9 **Double check** all your facts, making sure they are up to date. Editors trust their contributors to maintain a high standard of accuracy and you must always be reliable in every way if you want to go on selling your work.

10 **Keep on rewriting** making every sentence justify its place until you are satisfied that you have done all you can to improve the

article. Never say, 'Oh, I can't do it again!' Revision is essential, however tedious. It is always difficult to retain the original spontaneity while slaving to polish your work, but experience will gradually teach you how to do it. This is one of the greatest problems any writer has to face (see Chapter 12, Revision With Style.)

11 **Get some feedback:** If you belong to a writers' circle (and I strongly recommend it) now is the time to take your article along for criticism. You won't agree with every verdict but you will certainly receive some helpful advice. We all get so close to our work that we need a fresh opinion, especially after many hours of revision.

12 **Send a query letter** to the features' editor but only when you are certain you have a viable piece of writing. This letter should be brief and informative, outlining the subject matter, the length, the pictures you would provide and so on. If you have specialist knowledge on the subject you should say so here. The big advantage is that now, if you receive an encouraging response, you will be able to submit your article by return of post knowing that it is going to an interested editor rather than arriving cold and waiting for attention along with many, many others.

13 **Sending your work out.** When you feel that your article is ready for submission, type it in double spacing on A4 paper, following the advice laid down in Chapter 7, Presentation of Manuscripts. Pay great attention to detail; editors are highly professional people and they like their contributors to have an equally professional approach.

14 **Topical articles.** Be sure to submit a topical article in good time: two to three months ahead for a weekly magazine; four to six months for a monthly. I was surprised to learn, when I was a beginner, that some editors buy their Christmas articles in June.

Approaching an editor

Looking back over the list above, a professional writer with a publishing track record would have approached an editor after stage six, that is, having got the idea, identified a market, discovered the angle, planned the piece and decided what photographs would be needed. A freelance writer, known to the editor, might make first contact by telephone outlining the piece in less than 30 seconds to get the editor's approval and input on the idea at the earliest stage. I don't advise this early approach for beginners. It is better at this stage to encounter and overcome the problems which may arise in the course of writing the article well before you try to gain an editor's interest.

What about making email submissions or queries?

Don't. In the *Writers' and Artists' Yearbook 2002* over 60 per cent of the magazines listed for the UK and Ireland provide an email address but that is no more an invitation to make enquiries and submissions by email than the provision of a telephone number is an invitation to telephone the editor. If your article is accepted you may well be asked to submit changes etc and these will probably be sent by email at the editor's request. But until you are in that position, it's better to rely on the traditional methods for initial approaches.

Photographs

Changes in technology mean that many magazines will now consider colour and black and white prints rather than transparencies. Only 12 per cent of the magazines for UK and Ireland listed in the *Writers' and Artists' Yearbook* specify transparencies as their preferred medium. The quality of the prints, though, must be very high. Holiday snaps will not do for a travel article, for example. Submit prints only, never send negatives.

Photos must be glossy with plenty of contrast, and no smaller than half plate (16.5 cm × 12 cm, or 6.5 in × 4.75 in). Label them on the back with an adhesive address label and provide a functional caption including location, subject, etc. Don't write on the print itself, not even on the back. Use a fine, permanent marker rather than a ballpoint – the ink may smudge and rub onto the picture underneath. Provide the editor with a list of the photos/transparencies you have sent. Plastic folders may be used to display several photos on a sheet, helping to keep them together.

When to send photographs

Do not send photos or transparencies with your query letter but tell the editor what pictures are available. If you are sending the complete article unsolicited (not recommended) do not send photos but, again, let the editor know what pictures you have available. In any case, do not send original pictures but send copies in the first instance. It is much easier these days and relatively inexpensive to get copies. If the editor likes your article he will ask to see the pictures. Incidentally, if your photographs are used you should receive extra payment.

Digital photographs

Many home computer owners have already discovered how easy and how much fun it can be to use a digital camera and download the results onto a computer. The resulting images can then be edited, reduced, enlarged, enhanced, etc., before being printed out for the first time. Although computer printing inks and photographic paper are not cheap, you only need to print out those pictures which are up to standard. The digital format means that photos can be submitted on disk and viewed on the magazine publisher's computer where they can be further edited and enhanced. With the quality of digital cameras improving almost by the month – and costs coming down all the time, this medium will help the article/non-fiction writer immensely.

If you have high resolution digital pictures which could accompany your article then mention this to the editor early on, at the query letter stage, so that he is aware they are available. There are various file formats for digital pictures; jpeg is one of the most popular.

Copyright

The same rules of copyright apply to your pictures as to your words, that is, it will exist for 70 years after your death. It is therefore worth remembering that if you see just the right photograph to accompany your article, someone, somewhere will own the copyright, so it cannot be used without permission and probable payment of a fee. It's much simpler to learn the craft of photography and produce your own high quality pictures.

Illustrations

Don't attempt to draw your own illustrations, for example, line drawings, unless you are an exceptionally talented artist. Even then, you may find that your editor prefers to use his Art Department. Sketches and diagrams, however, could be useful for the guidance of a commissioned artist.

Payment

Fees vary a great deal, depending largely on the circulation of the magazine. Naturally, a well-known writer can claim a higher fee than a beginner, but otherwise payment is much the same for everyone, increasing if you become a regular contributor. Cheques are usually sent out after publication but some magazines pay on acceptance.

Some don'ts

Don't combine two or more subjects. This not only wastes material but spoils your article.

Don't preach.

Don't pad. If your article isn't long enough for the market, write it up for a different magazine or choose a subject with more 'meat' in it.

Don't repeat yourself. The reader will lose interest unless every sentence is new and fresh.

Don't be pessimistic. No one wants to feel dejected at the end of the article, and editors want to sell their magazines.

Don't hesitate to rewrite the whole article as many times as necessary.

Don't be discouraged by setbacks. Most writers have collected dozens of rejection slips by the time they reach the professional stage; one of my friends has actually papered the loo with them!

Exercise 6

Using the work you have done in Exercise 5 as a basis, research, plan and write an article which is appropriate in style and length for the market you have chosen.

Exercise 7

Write a humorous filler article of 400 words or less.

In this chapter you will learn:
- the scope of the modern short story
- the essential ingredients for a successful story
- how to create a good opening.

Nothing is wasted

It is very easy to write a bad short story – I know from experience. Although short stories require a different technique from novels, I realize now that those early failures were a necessary apprenticeship. It was through years of writing and rewriting – struggling to express myself clearly, to work out my plots, to bring the characters to life – that I learned the skills I needed to produce a full-length novel. None of our writing is wasted. There will be days when you feel that you haven't produced a single sentence to your satisfaction, but we all have those days and they are necessary to our development. Eventually we discover the form of writing we are best at – long or short, fiction or non-fiction, for children or for adults – but until we find that out, *all* our writing is valuable experience. Don't throw anything away! You never know when you may need odd paragraphs for reference or to include in some later story. I learnt my lesson when I had to empty the dustbin to retrieve a torn and crumpled page from the garbage.

Short stories can be any length from 500 to 2500 words, depending on the market, or up to 5000 words for writing competitions. An average of 850–1000 is a good 'canvas' for a story as it is a popular length with magazines.

Early efforts at writing can often produce results that are too macabre, too melodramatic. Beginners often find themselves drawn to write of suffering and violence, possibly because it is easier to create a dramatic effect in this way and, also, of course, to relieve their private griefs. The therapeutic value of creative writing should not be overlooked; getting our sorrows down on paper, disguised and reconstructed into fiction, can go a very long way towards removing them.

I kept on sending my early stories out and collecting rejection slips. Sometimes I had a letter to say that my work 'showed promise', but nobody told me what was wrong with it. Regrettably, editors haven't time for that. It wasn't until I joined a writers' circle that I began to see my mistakes and find out what really went into the making of a good short story. Of course, like most people who want to write them, I had read a great many, but reading for enjoyment is not enough; one must dissect, analyse, ask oneself questions. How did the story open? How and when was the main character introduced? What gave life to the setting? And what made the story *move*?

In the preface to his book *The Modern Short Story*, H. E. Bates says that 'it is the most difficult and exacting of all prose forms.'

This is generally accepted to be the case, and yet it is the form most commonly attempted by the beginner – and rightly so, because here he will be able to test his skills and learn his trade. He will learn the art of writing concisely, the swift but telling portrayal of character and the steady development towards a satisfying climax.

How, then, as a novice, are you to find the way to success? Here are the ingredients, as I see them, for a short story. Let's assume, to begin with, that you have a lively imagination and the ability to write grammatical prose; without these qualifications, short story writing is not for you. We will discuss the so-called 'straight' short story; fantasies, science fiction, children's stories and formula romances demand their own particular techniques, although most of the guidelines still apply. There is one ingredient which can hardly be listed, but if you can find it and add it to the others, your stories will acquire an extra quality. That ingredient is the magic in your mind: an innate sense of the wonder at the miracle of life, and of compassion for your fellow human beings. Without it you may write acceptable fiction but, in possession of that dimension, you can excel.

The ingredients

An original idea

Your idea may come to you 'out of the blue', a sudden inspiration while you sit on a train, wash the dishes or lie awake at night. On the other hand it may be sparked off by something that has happened to you, or by something you saw on television or read in a newspaper. Whatever it is, *it must excite you*. It must set you tingling with eagerness to get it down on paper. This idea is your theme. It answers that same question we asked ourselves back in Chapters 1 and 2 '*What am I trying to say?*' The events in your story (the plot), however interesting or dramatic, must also have significance. Even a light-hearted tale should reveal something important about human relationships.

Believable characters

Character, of course, is at the heart of all fiction (see Chapter 8, Characterization). A short story revolves around one central character whose problem will become of increasing interest. The reader must be made to feel at the outset that he knows and cares about this person, and you can best bring this about by the use of a single viewpoint throughout the story – that is, *seeing everything through that one person's eyes*. I believe that it is vital to stay in the mind of your central character, that is, the viewpoint character, from the first word to the last. Stories are published which ignore this rule, but when you are a beginner you should adhere to it very strictly. Later you may occasionally decide to switch viewpoint character in order to create a special effect, but you will then understand exactly what you are doing and why you are doing it.

Be sure to choose the right central character. Ask yourself, before you plan your story: whose problem is it? If in doubt, choose the character with whom you sympathize. Unless *you* care, your reader will not care.

First person or third? This is always a difficult decision; it depends on the story and on your own individual approach to the theme and the situation. The first person is probably easier to write, as one can identify more readily with an 'I' character, and emotions can be expressed more naturally. And of course there are no viewpoint problems.

Dialogue is essential: people reveal themselves by the things they say, and the reader, hearing the voices of your characters, will feel that he knows them. 'He often spoke unkindly to his wife' is far less effective than a scene in which you show the two of them together and let us hear exactly what he says to her and in what circumstances. In other words, choose direct narrative whenever possible, painting a vivid picture of a particular occasion, rather than making generalizations.

Although you will have to bring your characters to life in a few words, you need not deny yourself the luxury of the memorable phrase, the original observation. Descriptions can be concise yet richly evocative; this is a part of your craft.

A convincing background

Your characters should move in a realistic setting, briefly evoked like the characters themselves. Atmosphere is of great importance. You must take the reader into an imaginary world, make him believe in it, and do so *at once* (see Chapter 10, Setting).

You would be wise to choose the kind of setting you know; not necessarily a real place, of course, but somewhere you can picture in your mind's eye without difficulty. Lighting is important, as well as movement – a sudden flash of sunlight on a water jug, the shadow of a man across a cobbled street, the swaying of willow branches reflected in water. You can only bring these things to life for the reader if you can see them with the inner eye of your imagination.

Pay attention to sounds and smells, as well as the way things look. Fiction writing demands the use of all our senses.

A good opening

You should introduce your main character without delay, expressing his *feelings* and avoiding long descriptions and explanations. There is probably something wrong with your story if, by the bottom of page 2, you have failed to introduce your main character, state his/her problem *and* establish an intriguing situation. I attach great importance to the first two pages. Here you must arouse your reader's curiosity or run the risk of losing him for ever. It's no use having a brilliant scene on page four if nobody gets that far!

Conflict

No short story can exist without conflict. Your central character must be faced with a problem at the outset; it may be in the shape of a person, a decision, ambition, dread, the forces of nature or of war, but no story will hold the reader's attention unless there is some kind of early confrontation. Contented people are hopelessly unsuitable material for fiction; sadly, there is no drama in peace and happiness!

Suspense

Suspense and plot are closely connected. Having set the scene with your main character in a situation of conflict, your object is to maintain momentum until the end. Readability, an essential quality in any kind of writing, depends on beguiling the reader into turning the page; this means that the interest must never flag, that you must stick to the main story line and build up inexorably to the final climax. This by no means implies that your story must be packed with dangerous dilemmas and breathless drama. A delicate atmospheric story can be equally enthralling if you build up the tension in the mind of your viewpoint character. A state of anxiety, if we care about the person, can provide unbearable suspense. (Does he love her? How will so-and-so react? When will the telephone ring?) With practice you will learn to think in terms of dramatic situations, discarding the trivial and the tedious, and commanding the reader's unswerving attention.

If you are worried about 'plotting' you will find it helpful to build on the first dramatic situation. Every scene will suggest another scene; it's as if each confrontation lights an explosive charge which ignites the next one. You might be able to plan the whole story before you begin – and it's advisable, if you can – but many writers develop the action as they go along, finding inspiration in the dilemmas of their characters. Suspense, whether subtle and low key or of great intensity, is the very life-blood of successful fiction. You are inventing a piece of life but, unlike real life, your story must have an artistic form, a framework to hold it tightly together. And this brings us to the next ingredient, shape.

Shape

Quite simply, this means a beginning, a middle and an end. There is no substitute for sound construction, although you may choose to develop your story along unconventional lines.

In general terms, the beginning introduces the characters, sets the scene and poses the problem; the middle develops the action and involves the reader in a situation of increasing fascination; and the end resolves the problem, for better or worse. Be sure that everything is relevant to your theme. Be ruthless in pruning away all superfluous incidents, descriptions, even characters. And keep your time span fairly short, avoiding spaces to denote the passage of weeks or months. A single problem and a single period of time will give your story that tautness of construction which is so important. Once you have brought it to a conclusion, don't extend it into anti-climax with needless explanations. Let it speak for itself.

A satisfying ending

The ending need not be a happy one. It's enough for us to nod our heads, wisely and sadly, saying to ourselves, 'Yes that's life!' A totally happy ending is seldom satisfying to the discerning reader because it is not convincing; life doesn't work like that. The best endings are unexpected but inevitable, so that we look up from the final word and gasp 'Of course!' Some stories leave us thinking 'Oh, *no!*' (the contrived), or 'So what? (the banal). I like a note of hope in my short story endings, as I do with plays and novels – the feeling that the main character has been through some difficult times but has emerged in a better position to face the future. Am I saying, then, that your hero or heroine should not be permitted to die? Yes, I think I am. The death of the hero, with whom the reader has identified, comes like a little death for him as well. And there is another point. You may have heard the anecdote about the man who nodded off to sleep in a chair and dreamed he was an aristocrat in the French Revolution with his head on the block waiting for the guillotine to descend. Someone tapped him on the back of the neck with a book at the precise moment when the blade fell, and the shock caused the man to die in his sleep.

Aha, but in that case, how could anyone have known about the dream? The same problem arises if you allow your viewpoint character to die.

The art of fiction is a strange deceit; the author tells us lies as if they were true, and yet there is a kind of integrity behind the make-believe, a sense of what is acceptable and what is not.

Some classic openings

The following openings demonstrate how the authors have launched the story, created an atmosphere and introduced the main character at the same time. When you have learned to intermingle characterization, setting and action, you have mastered one of the most important techniques of fiction writing. Here are a few examples beginning with Roald Dahl:

Down below there was only a vast white undulating sea of cloud. Above there was the sun, and the sun was white like clouds, because it is never yellow when one looks at it from high in the air.

He was still flying the Spitfire. His right hand was on the stick and he was working the rudder-bar with his left leg alone. It was quite easy. The machine was flying well. He knew what he was doing.

Everything is fine, he thought. I'm doing all right. I'm doing nicely. I know my way home. I'll be there in half an hour. When I land I shall taxi in and switch off my engine and I shall say, help me to get out, will you. I shall make my voice sound ordinary and natural and none of them will take any notice. Then I shall say, someone help me to get out. I can't do it alone because I've lost one of my legs. They'll all laugh and think I'm joking and I shall say, all right, come and have a look, you unbelieving bastards. Then Yorky will climb up on to the wing and look inside. He'll probably be sick because of all the blood and the mess. I shall laugh and say, for God's sake, help me get out.

Beware of the Dog by Roald Dahl

The telephone rang beside the bed in the middle of the night and she woke struggling across her husband's body to grab the receiver. Their movements under the bedclothes might have denoted mating or fighting; the fact was that even in sleep she was alert to the humiliation of hearing him answer the telephone without teeth in his mouth.

A Mad One by Nadine Gordimer

He simply said my name. He said, 'Martha', and once again I could feel it happening. My legs trembled under the big white cloth and my head became fuzzy, though I was not drunk. It's how I fall in love. He sat opposite. The love object. Elderly. Blue eyes. Khaki hair.

The Love Object by Edna O'Brien

It began with the voices, the sound of muttering that pressed up against the back of her neck, as though the voices were hands that grasped and stroked her, raising gooseflesh. After a little, the voices ceased quarrelling and sank away to a whisper, to be replaced by an unnerving solo, a thin, high, wavering humming that went on and on, until Clothilde sat up in the darkness and cried out and the unearthly humming stopped.

A Story for Hallowe'en by Michèle Roberts

The following extract from Nadine Gordimer's introduction to her own *Selected Stories* will give you a foretaste of the possibilities which await you when you begin this beguiling task. 'A short story occurs in the imaginative sense. To write one is to express from a situation in the exterior or interior world the life-giving drop – sweat, tear, semen, saliva – that will spread in intensity on the page; burn a hole in it.' (Note her delightful use of the word 'express'.)

Exercise 8

Choose a theme and central character for a short story. Make notes for a beginning, middle and end, and write the first 500 words. (One of your previous exercises may form a good basis.)

the magazine short story

In this chapter you will learn:
- how to identify markets for your fiction
- how to analyze published stories
- how to establish your characters and conflict in your opening paragraph.

The magazine market is highly competitive and success, therefore, is quite difficult to achieve. However, it can be done, particularly if you discover that you already have the right skills or can develop them. Those skills include devising a tight plot and moving it along at a fast pace using dialogue and characterization to foster both interest and reader identification with the main character. All this in less than 1000 words – and sometimes as little as 750! It's a highly skilled task and yet some new writers take to it naturally and achieve early success.

In the main, magazine fiction means women's fiction as featured in the weekly and monthly titles. Here, there is demand for a wide range of stories from family stories to ghost, crime, mystery and twist-ending tales, plus stories featuring animals and children and 'starring' viewpoint characters of all ages. In recent years many of the major weekly magazines have introduced fiction specials devoted entirely to stories, for example, *Woman's Weekly Fiction Special* (every two months) and *Take a Break's Fiction Feast*, (monthly). Many magazines also issue seasonal specials – Spring, Summer and Autumn and these usually include fiction.

Researching the magazine fiction market

A magazine survives by identifying its readership, providing what the readership wants and attracting advertisers who want to promote their products. If you wish to take part in this endeavour you, too, must know who that reader is and consider whether or not you can write for that sector of the market. If you are insincere, thinking you can dash off 1000 word formulaic romance without market research and study, it will show. Not to the reader, who will never get to see the story, but to the editor.

No two magazines are exactly alike even though they may be rivals operating within the same sector. There are subtle differences and these will become apparent only after a period of study and comparison. If you did jump to the conclusion that a romance is just what the fiction editor is waiting for then this only underlines the importance of market research. Romances are by no means the norm in magazine fiction and haven't been for many years. However, a good romance which manages to be that little bit different and fresh will always sell to the right market whether the writer was established before or not.

Unsolicited manuscripts

Not every magazine carrying fiction will consider an 'unsolicited manuscript', that is one which has been sent in by an unknown author speculatively without invitation or query. Check the particular title you have in mind in the *Writers' and Artists' Yearbook* or *The Writer's Handbook* first to see what the magazine's policy is before you go any further with your research.

Studying the magazine: what to look for

One of the key factors in magazine fiction is *reader identification.* It's something the fiction editor will look for in your story, asking the question, 'Will our readers identify with this main character and her situation?' In order to be able to pass the 'test' you must gain an accurate impression of that particular title's reader. Fortunately there are a number of fairly reliable indicators in the magazine itself which can help you to gauge their lifestyle, age, interests and hobbies.

The advertisements

What products are on offer? Whom are the products aimed at? It's worth remembering that the advertiser will have paid a lot of money for the space in the magazine and will have a clear idea of the reader.

The features

Look at the range of subjects covered. As we have seen in Chapter 3, the successful features will be those which the editor feels are of greatest interest to the readership.

Is there a fashion page?

If so look at the models and the age range the clothes are intended for. The price of the clothes is another useful indicator.

Readers' letters page

The letters usually provide a warm and often light-hearted glimpse of the regular readership – although not always. Serious issues are raised here too, especially in response to past features. It's one more reason why you should study several copies of the magazine as part of your market research, so you can keep up to date with the trends in the magazine.

The problems page

You can gain an insight here into some of the problems readers face. Studying this page over a period of time will help to give you an idea of the territory of the magazine and possibly provide the inspiration or theme for a story.

Analyzing the stories

Study the main character

Whose story is it? Let's assume the main character is female (this is not always so but for the majority of stories it holds true). Make a note of how old she is. What her job is. Is she married or single, engaged or divorced? What problem or source of conflict does she face? Is the reader meant to be sympathetic or unsympathetic towards her? How is the problem resolved?

Style

The picture illustrating the story will give you (and the reader) a lot of advance knowledge about the main character and the story setting. You may also discover that, because of the illustration, there is no need for the author to describe the character at all. Look closely, too, at the opening paragraph to see how quickly the story gathers pace. Note the use of dialogue and how it helps to characterize and develop the main protagonists whilst moving the story forwards. Notice the length of the sentences and the vocabulary and style of language used.

Story presentation

How many pages does the story occupy? Single page, double page or more? Is this a regular story slot or just a one-off? Roughly how many words? Can you categorize the story? Could you say, in one sentence, what the story was really about, for example, this is the story of how one sister sought to gain revenge over the other; or this is the story of how one sister finally came to understand the actions of the other. What was the theme – revenge or communication? Did the twists and turns of the plot feature most in the story or was it the emotional interaction of the characters? There is much to be learned from studying magazine fiction, not least the variety and high quality that is on offer.

Some magazines provide helpful guidelines for fiction writers, for example, *Woman's Weekly*, *My Weekly*, *Woman*, *The People's Friend* and *The Lady*. This further underlines their willingness to encourage new writers and to ensure that the manuscripts they receive are closer to their requirements than at present. Whilst it is true that magazines receive many hundreds of manuscripts a month, all competing for the same few story slots, it is also true that the vast majority of those manuscripts are miles off target. The reason most frequently cited by editors is that the author had not done sufficient market research into the current needs of the magazine.

You will require great skill and discipline to become a magazine fiction writer plus a lot of determination and a little luck too, but if this is your chosen field, hard work and persistence together with your flair and talent will eventually see you through.

Subject matters

Family stories are popular, perhaps concentrating on a particular relationship – mother and daughter; mother and son; father and son – as well as on the kinds of problems most families encounter at one stage or another. Stories featuring children in a major role, perhaps even as the viewpoint character, are difficult to pull off but if you can achieve it you could stand a strong chance with the right magazine.

Twist-in-the-tale stories include a great variety of story types, for example, crime, ghost, humour, mystery. These, too, are very difficult to pull off especially as they are usually less than 1000 words. Trying to outwit a reader who knows in advance there is going to be a twist is no easy task. Ideally the twist should come in the last paragraph or, better still, the last line!

Relationship stories – about friendship, work-related problems, romances, if, as I noted above, you can bring something fresh to the genre.

Animal stories – *not* stories taking the viewpoint of an animal – these are rarely accepted – but instead those where animals feature as part of the family/work setting and play an important character role in the story.

Some classic openings

Note how quickly author Jackie Winter establishes character, setting and problem all within the first 220 words of her 1000 word story, *The Ugly Baby*.

Maggie watched the other mums on the ward. They all looked thrilled with their babies. Beautiful was the word she kept hearing. Every precious bundle was so, so beautiful.

Maggie cradled Joe in her arms. He was almost asleep. Small face solemn, wise and mysterious. Faint purple smudges beneath tightly closed eyes. He was adorable and she loved him. Maggie gulped. Loved him, in spite of the fact that he was quite definitely the ugliest baby she'd ever seen.

How could she feel like that about her own child? She'd often thought other people's babies were fairly hideous. Gone into hypocritical raptures to satisfy their doting parents.

Surely love was supposed to be blind? Which must mean all women were programmed to think their babies were gorgeous. So why wasn't that magic working for her? It was quite obvious to Maggie that Joe was ugly. The ugliest baby on the ward.

Even her mother thought so. Not that she'd admit it. But it was the words she didn't use which rang most loudly in Maggie's ears.

'Will you give him a bath when he wakes up? He loves his bath, doesn't he? Such a good baby.'

Her mum hovered over the cot and Maggie sighed. A good baby, she thought, dismally. Good, not beautiful.

The Ugly Baby by Jackie Winter, published by *Woman* magazine

In Della Galton's story, *One Step Ahead*, dialogue features from the opening line and, once again, characters, setting and problem are established within the first 300 words of her 1000 word story.

'What did you say you were looking for?' John lowered the newspaper for a second, but I knew he wasn't really listening. His mind was still on the football results.

'I told you. Something for the dinner dance on Saturday.'

'Mmm,' he said. 'I can't believe we lost at home.'

'The only criteria,' I continued dreamily, 'is that it must be size twelve.'

From the other side of the table, Adam, who's going through the *'aren't parents stupid'* stage, gave an unflattering snort of laughter.

I glared at him. 'I *am* size twelve.'

'In your dreams Mum.'

'Well I was the last time I went shopping for a dress.'

'The last time you bought a dress, I was still in the Scouts,' Adam said. 'We've had four Christmases since then.'

When I thought about it, I had to admit that he might have a point. I wasn't exactly a 'dress' type of person. I worked from home and tended to live in jogging bottoms and baggy sweatshirts. And those elasticated waistbands are very forgiving. Not, of course, that I was going to admit it to the two males in my life. Both of whom are irritatingly tall and slim and can eat whatever they like without putting on an ounce.

'Of course I'm still a size twelve,' I said crossly.

'What do you reckon Dad?' Adam said and then when he got no response, 'Hey Mum – bet you a fiver you don't buy one single thing that size.'

'Don't be ridiculous. I'm not betting you anything.'

'Coward,' he challenged.

'All right – a fiver. And if you lose you can clear out the shed – like you promised to about six weeks ago.'

'No problem.' We shook hands and he grinned. He looked awfully confident.

One Step Ahead by Della Galton, published by *People's Friend*

Things you won't find in a magazine short story

Bad language, racial stereotypes, sexually explicit scenes, cruelty, abuse, violence and horror.

Exercise 9

Use the 'What to look for' market research guidelines above to identify a target market which appeals to you. Analyse the fiction and write a synopsis of each story limiting yourself to 30 words maximum per story. Let each story summary begin with the words, 'This is the story of...'

Competitions

There are a few annual magazine short story competitions to look out for as part of your on-going market research. News of them is usually posted on the cover. These competitions often exclude published writers in the rules – further proof that there is a real willingness to find new talent. Here are a few to look out for:

The Lady **Annual Short Story Competition** – with £1000 prize plus publication to the winner, plus runner-up prizes. Details announced in the first issue in October of this highly respected weekly magazine. Subjects/themes for the competition change each year. The maximum number of words is 2000.

Good Housekeeping – annual competition offering talented, unpublished authors the chance to win £1000 plus publication. There are a number of runner-up prizes on offer too.

Woman's Own – annual short story competition encouraging new writers. Usually 1000 words maximum.

Woman and Home – highly regarded short story competition. Maximum words usually 2000 with excellent prizes including cash and publication. Watch for details late in the autumn.

Woman's Weekly – famed for its fiction, *Woman's Weekly* is always worth researching. Occasional competitions (including poetry competitions, too).

Sending your work out

For a detailed look at how your final draft should appear see Chapter 7, Presentation of manuscripts. Always enclose a self-addressed envelope of the correct size and with the correct postage. It is not necessary to use recorded delivery or registered post. Opinions differ between fiction editors regarding the need for a covering letter accompanying the manuscript. Most say this is not necessary but others, for example, *Woman's Weekly* fiction editor, Gaynor Davies, prefers to know a *little* about the author. However, the lack of a covering letter won't affect your story's chances.

Don't expect a comment from the fiction editor but if you do get one take serious note of it. If an editor rejects your story but asks for more then consider it as a near-miss and try harder!

Don't phone, fax or email the magazine regarding your story. Be patient. It can take up to three months for your story to make it to the top of the pile for consideration.

Don't submit to more than one title at a time.

Don't let your market research lapse once you have done it. It's a continuous process.

Useful website

The Jacqui Bennett Writers Bureau (www.jbwb.co.uk) offers individual links to the writers' guidelines mentioned above and much more besides. There are market pages for stories and articles as well as the novel and the non-fiction book plus listings of competitions for short stories and poetry. UK publishers and literary agents are listed and there are links to market information covering the US, Australia and New Zealand and a whole host of other writers' resources available on the Web.

Exercise 10

Write the opening 300 words of a magazine story establishing character, problem and setting. You could use the situation mentioned above – two sisters struggling to communicate – as the basis for your story.

creative writing competitions

In this chapter you will learn:
- how to choose the right competition for your work
- how to avoid competition pitfalls
- which are the leading UK competitions.

As we have seen, the highly competitive magazine market offers opportunities, albeit quite difficult ones, for certain types of stories aimed at a specific audience. But what if the kind of story you are burning to write doesn't happen to be suitable for a magazine audience?

There are many national (and international) creative writing competitions aimed at the poet and short story writer, plus a relatively rare few catering for article/non-fiction writers, novelists and playwrights. Competitions can vary in quality – some are nothing more than fund-raisers while others have a genuine literary standing, for example, The Bridport Prize (short stories and poems) and The Cardiff International Poetry Competition.

Entering writing competitions

You should research a competition just as thoroughly as you would a market. Not only will this help you to gauge the integrity of the competition but it should give you a better chance of doing well in it.

How to research a writing competition

The following checklist will help you to avoid some of the pitfalls:

1 Write to the Competition Secretary for the rules of entry even if an entry form is not required. Always enclose a stamped addressed envelope when requesting information.

2 Check the rules of entry with particular reference to the following:

a Copyright should remain with the author whether the entry is successful in the competition or not. However, some competitions stipulate that the copyright in the winning stories/poems is temporarily 'licensed' to the competition for a fixed period after the results are known. After this period elapses full copyright reverts back to the author. This is generally acceptable as it allows the organizers to use the story in an anthology or quotes from it in subsequent publicity. Transferring all rights in the piece on a permanent basis is not acceptable.

b Check what happens to the unsuccessful manuscripts if they are not returned to the author.

c Check who is eligible to enter the competition – some competitions exclude previously published authors.

3   If a website address is given, visit the site and obtain as much information as you can.

4   Who will judge the competition? If judging is to be carried out by a writers' circle then it is worth doing a little research to find out when they were established, how large the group is etc. If the judge is named and you are not familiar with his or her work, a trip to the bookshop or library should help. Alternatively, visit one of the online bookshops and make use of their search facilities.

5   When was the competition established? Does it have a good reputation?

6   How many of the total entries will the judge get to see? This may be harder to find out but it is as well to be aware that, sometimes, the celebrity judge sees only a shortlist of entries – perhaps 50 or less. If this is so who decides on the shortlist? Probably the writers' group/sponsor.

7   Compare the entry fee to the prize money on offer, for example, a £10 entry fee set against a £50 first prize is obviously an extreme example but the principle is valid. There should also be a number of runner-up prizes.

8   How and when will the winners be notified? Knowing this date will tell you when the story can safely be sent elsewhere.

9   What is the length required – is there a minimum as well as a maximum? Never exceed the number of words you have been set – not even by one word!

10 Is there a set theme for the competition? The way that you interpret the theme could get your manuscript noticed but, on the other hand, your interpretation shouldn't be so obscure as to flirt with disqualification!

11 How should the manuscript be presented? Follow the requirements exactly regarding manuscript presentation and don't assume that all competitions have the same requirements.

12 Most competitions are judged anonymously, that is the author's name does not appear on the manuscript itself but only on the title page. So if you are submitting an old story that has already been to a magazine, for example, it will have to be printed out/typed again. If you want your manuscript to look its best, blanking out your name at the top and/or bottom of each page with sticky paper is not an option.

13 Be aware that some competitions ask for more than one copy of your entry to be submitted. This enables two 'readers' to have a copy of the story at the same time in the process of assembling a short list.

14 Most competitions do not return manuscripts once the judging has been completed, in which case it is a waste of time sending a self-addressed envelope.

Some dos and don'ts

Don't try to make amendments after you have entered the manuscript no matter how vital they may seem.

Don't leave your entry until the last minute.

Don't send an old story out unless you have re-read it, reconsidered it and possibly rewritten it in the light of the new audience you hope to be addressing – and the further experience you will have gained since you wrote it.

Do try to read some of the past winning entries to the competition. Sometimes an anthology is available covering previous winners. This will help you to assess the quality of the competition and whether or not you are on the same wavelength as the organizers!

Do be patient at every stage of this process: when you are researching which competition to enter, when you are writing or selecting the story/poem to enter, when you are editing and polishing your entry. Success may not be immediate but when it comes you will have the satisfaction of having been judged the best.

Competition writing versus magazine writing

Competitions: advantages and disadvantages

Advantages include:

- working to a deadline
- greater creative scope
- longer length to explore characterization, setting etc.

Disadvantages include:

- an entry fee
- having to work with a set theme
- the fact that entries are not usually returned
- reliance on the integrity of the organizers in smaller competitions.

Magazines: advantages and disadvantages

Advantages include:

- clearly defined readership
- a huge audience
- good discipline promoting good habits
- focused story and length
- good pay (generally speaking).

Disadvantages include:

- highly competitive market
- rejection slips can be disheartening
- relatively few story slots.

A classic opening

Here is the opening of Della Galton's story *Better Eyes* which was a quarterly winner in the *World Wide Writers* short story competition. The story is just under 3000 words in length but its opening illustrates how characterization, atmosphere and setting can all be explored without holding up the development of the story.

> The first time I saw her, it was as a blur in the headlights of my car. A white Alsatian, or possibly a very light, golden retriever. Sodden from the rain, her ears flattened against her head, her four white legs going like pistons. I braked too hard, skidding on the wet road, but I didn't hit her. My immediate impression was that she was running in terror, although, not in terror of my car.
>
> She was heading towards the cemetery behind the church. Almost ghost like, but too wet for a ghost. I hesitated, then pulled over, one wheel bumping up onto the pavement. It was not a night for heroics, but I've always had a soft spot for dogs and this one was in trouble.
>
> I opened the door reluctantly. To my right, the spire of the church loomed, a darker silhouette against the night. The wind slapped the rain across it, with as little respect as the sea, for a lifeboat, in a storm. I turned my head to see that the rain-washed clock face put the time at just before midnight. Not the sort of time to take a stroll around a cemetery, yet if I didn't go, I knew I would always wonder. Dragging a raincoat from the back of the car, I headed in the direction she had gone.

'Here beauty,' I called, as I walked. More for the reassurance of my own voice than in any hope of a response. She (and for some reason I was sure it was a she) had been going like the clappers. No reason to think she'd slow down for me.

At least she'd be easy to spot. White as she was. One quick look and if I didn't see her I would go. Back to the warmth of my car, the warmth of Jan at home. Would Jan still be up? I thought she would. She often forgot the time when she was writing. Radiators blasting away; REM whining in the background; a brandy sitting on the mantelpiece for me; her own black coffee at her elbow. She never drank when she was writing. Said it was a poor show if it took a bottle of red wine to get your inhibitions off the page. It was a nice picture. I kept it with me, a little corner of warmth in my mind as the headstones came into view.

Note the contrast between the two settings enabling the reader to 'see' where he is heading even before he has arrived. And the dog? Well she is of course one of the major strands of the story. For more on Characterization see Chapter 8 and on Setting see Chapter 10.

Short story and poetry outlets

Although short story and poetry collections by established writers are quite a common sight in major bookshops, it is unlikely that a publisher would consider a collection by a single unknown author. The financial investment required and the risks involved in publishing a book are too great for this to be a likely proposition.

Small press publications and magazines listed in *The Writer's Handbook* show alternative outlets for fiction of varying lengths and genres together with poetry ranging from the experimental to the traditional. Payment is generally low if there is a payment at all, and the audience is probably as specialized as it is in the mainstream market, so market research is just as essential here to identify the right audience for your work.

A short selection of established writing competitions

The Bridport Prize
Bridport Arts Centre, South Street, Bridport, Dorset DT6 3NR.
www.bridportprize.org.uk
Short story and poetry categories. Closes end of June each year.
Prize: £3000.

Writers Bureau Poetry and Short Story Competition
Established 1994.
The Writers Bureau, Sevendale House, 7 Dale Street,
Manchester M1 1JB.
www.writersbureau.com
Closing date end of July. Prize £1000.

Arvon Foundation International Poetry Competition
Established 1980.
11 Westbourne Crescent, London W2 3DB
www.arvonfoundation.org
email: london@arvonfoundation.org
Biennial competition (even numbered years). Prize £5000.

Cardiff International Poetry Competition
Established 1986.
PO Box 438, Cardiff CF10 5YA.
www.academi.org
email: post@academi.org
Closes in June each year. Prize pool: £5000.

The National Poetry Competition (in association with BT)
The Poetry Society, 22 Betterton Street, London WC2H 9BX.
www.poetrysoc.com
email info@poetrysoc.com
Prize: £5000.

Sid Chaplin Short Story Competition
Established 1986.
Shildon Town Council, Civic Centre Square, Shildon, Co
Durham DL4 1AH.
Annual short story competition, usually themed. Entry forms
available from September each year. Closing date end of
December. Prize: £300.

Kent Short Story Competition
Established 1992.
Kent Literature Festival, The Metropole Arts Centre, The Leas,
Folkestone, Kent CT20 2LS.
Entry forms available from March each year. Prize: £350.

Useful website

The Book Trust provides a comprehensive A–Z of annual awards and prizes. Visit www.booktrust.org.uk

---

Exercise 11

The themes below have been used in various competitions in recent years. Choose one theme only and, with reference to the list of 'ingredients' outlined in Chapter 4, experiment with various possible approaches to the theme before writing a beginning to the story. Your beginning should be no more than 300 words.

Themes

Sin, the family, water, music, farewell, travelling light.

presentation of manuscripts

In this chapter you will learn:
- how to set out your title page
- how to set out your manuscript for submission to an editor
- the importance of protecting your copyright.

General advice

It cannot be too strongly emphasized that your typescript must be impeccable. I have seen a short story which was sent to an editor on flimsy little sheets of blue notepaper, handwritten in purple ink and fastened together with a *pin*! Such extremes are rare, thank goodness, but many beginners send out their manuscripts in an unbelievably shoddy state. You have put a great deal of work into your writing and it would be madness not to take equal care with its presentation. It's easy to get it right when you understand the requirements and even easier now that the computer can automate many of the settings and margins etc.

A manuscript, in official jargon, is the same thing as a typescript/hard copy, even though the word 'manuscript' implies that it is written by hand. MS = manuscript, plural = MSS. Likewise, p. = page, plural = pp.

Page layout

Use good, standard quality A4 paper (297 mm × 210 mm). You should allow a good margin on the left-hand side (not less than 40 mm with at least 25 mm top and bottom and 13 mm on the right. Be sure that your margins are consistent throughout.

Use one side of the paper only and type in double spacing – that is, leave a blank line between each line of text. (It is advisable to use this same double spacing for your rough draft/print outs as well, to simplify revision; it is almost impossible to make amendments and additions if the work is single spaced.)

It is neither necessary nor desirable to allow extra spacing between paragraphs. Details such as these are by no means vital to your success as a writer, but it's just as easy to be accurate so why not let your typescript proclaim your general efficiency?

It is usual to indent five spaces for a new paragraph and to allow two spaces after a full stop. Be sure to number your pages, preferably in the top right-hand corner, and check that they are in the correct order.

If your manuscript includes headings (most likely in a non-fiction title) be sure to differentiate between main and sub-headings. For example, use upper case for a main heading, bold for a sub-heading and italic for a minor heading. This helps to avoid any unnecessary confusion at the editing stage.

Always keep a copy of your work. Backup your computer files regularly. Keep up-to-date copies. When you are working on a computer save your work every few minutes or adjust the settings to ensure this is done automatically.

Draft copies

If you are using a computer it is advisable to print out your work and make pencil corrections on the 'hard copy'. Why? Something very mysterious happens between the 'perfect' version you see on the screen and the one you see on the paper. Suddenly the missing full stops, the extra spaces, the false paragraphs etc all catch your eye – now they are on the page. Use scrap paper, save your work, print it out, shut your computer down and take your draft somewhere quiet where you can concentrate and make your corrections.

The title page

The title page should bear your name, address, telephone number and email address (if you have one) at the top right-hand side. About half way down comes the title in capitals and under that the 'by-line'. This is where you give your pseudonym if you want to use one, but I don't advise it unless you have a special reason for not using your real name; it only complicates matters.

At the bottom of the page state the approximate number of words. As we have already seen, there is no need to count every word except for very short pieces. Take an average of ten lines, count the number of lines on a page and multiply one by the other. Never state the exact number of words; give it to the nearest hundred for articles and short stories, to the nearest thousand for full-length books. If an editor sees '2832 words' he will know at once that you are a beginner.

Articles and short stories

FBSRO

When you submit stories and articles to magazines in the UK you should also state at the bottom of your title page: 'First British Serial Rights Offered' (FBSRO). This indicates that you are *not* prepared to sell the copyright but only the right to publish the piece once only, for the first time in Great Britain. After a few

Joan Smith
49, Nowhere Place,
TOLLINGTON,
Sussex. 0XX 0XX

Tel: (00000 000000)

Email: joan.smith@isp.com

FIVE HUNDRED MILES OF CANAL

by

Joan Smith

Approx. 1500 words   F.B.S.R. offered

specimen layout for the title page of an article or short story years you might be able to sell the *Second* British Serial Rights, but when offering second rights always state when and where the material was first published. An article already published in a magazine can sometimes be rewritten as a radio talk from a different angle. FBSRO wouldn't apply here because the BBC has its own terms of contract.

The copyright of all your work belongs to you, as the author, unless you agree to sell it (see Chapter 24, The Professional Approach). This you should seldom do. Your short story, for instance, may be spotted in a magazine by a film or television company (unlikely but possible) and if you had sold the copyright, the magazine which bought it would get all the money and you might never even know about it.

If you are sent a letter or a cheque which implies the purchase of 'the copyright' or 'all rights' simply cross it out and substitute 'FBSRO'. You may wish to query this via a telephone call to find out what the publications terms are. If you find yourself put in a situation where if you don't accept the terms you won't get published – think very hard indeed before going ahead. Copyright is even more precious than publication.

The first page of the manuscript

This must bear your name, address and email address if you have one in the top right-hand corner. (The title sheet is removed and sent to the Accounts Department if your MS is accepted, hence the need for the duplicated information.) A quarter of the way down the page, type the title and the by-line once again, leave a double-double space, indent five spaces and begin your article or story.

Your name or the title should appear at the top of every page in case the sheets come adrift, and it is a good idea to repeat your name and address on the last page of the MS.

When your manuscript is ready

Fasten the pages together with a paper clip. On no account fold the manuscript more than once (it is really best to pack your work flat). Always enclose a stamped, self-addressed envelope of the right size. A very brief covering letter is all that is required; your earlier query letter will have given the editor all the information he needs. If, at the request of the editor, you are enclosing photographs, provide a list of the enclosures (See Chapter 3,

Joan Smith
49, Nowhere Place,
TOLLINGTON,
Sussex 0XX 0XX

FIVE HUNDRED MILES OF CANAL

by

Joan Smith

'Fancy going in winter!' they said. But that was the way we wanted it. In a tiny cruiser last year, my husband and I covered five hundred miles of the canals of England – from London to Manchester and back – and we found a new country.

We wanted to discover the 'Cut' alone, without the transistors and the orange peel of the holiday season. Frosts and snows whitened the roof of our little craft as we nosed our way slowly from lock to lock, from town to town, sometimes hacking a channel through stretches of ice.

We shared those lonely reaches with ony the narrow-boats, still chugging along with their various cargoes, and the calm, unhurried scene might have belonged to the 19th Century. Between the towns, the canal passed through forests and fields, over tall aqueducts, through dark dripping tunnels, and sometimes ran along the ridge of a hill so that

specimen layout of the first page of an article or short story

How to Write an Article). Short stories seldom require a covering letter. Find out the name of the person you are sending it to – Features editor or Fiction editor. The *Writers' and Artists' Yearbook* or *The Writer's Handbook* may be able to help here but if not, a phone call to the switchboard of the publication concerned should provide the information.

Never send the same piece to two markets at the same time. This is totally unethical and your name will be black-listed if you do so. Allow at least two months for a reply. If you receive no news in that time, write politely to ask if they have reached a decision.

By the time your manuscript has been to several magazines it will begin to look untidy. Print out another copy. Never submit a manuscript which is anything but clean and neat. Creased pages, tea stains (editors are great tea and coffee drinkers) or curled-up corners will ruin your chances. A protective extra sheet of paper at the back can help.

Be sure you don't send out a manuscript with the last rejection slip still attached. It has been done!

Finally, it is advisable to keep a special notebook to record the comings and goings of your manuscripts. The book can be ruled into columns with 'Title; Where sent; Date sent; Date returned; Remarks; Fee paid'. It's a great day when you first fill in that right-hand column! It isn't just the cheque that delights you — it's the knowledge that an editor is prepared to buy your work. He thinks it is well written and that his readers will enjoy it. All your efforts have been worthwhile.

Exercise 12

Complete any one of the exercises you have tried so far and produce a final draft following the advice given above.

---

part

two

writing techniques

characterization

In this chapter you will learn:
- how to create believable characters
- the importance of choosing the right name for your character
- how to develop your characters.

Creating believable characters

'To write fiction,' said Aldous Huxley, 'one needs a whole series of inspirations about people in an environment, and then a whole lot of hard work on the basis of those inspirations.'

Your characters must come to life as full-blooded individuals with strong emotions, authentic talk and convincing reactions to every situation if your work is to satisfy the reader. In order to create such characters you must get to know them very well indeed. This means thinking about them deeply, searching out their secret fears and longings, standing back from them without judging, yet also, paradoxically, identifying with them even though they are quite different from yourself.

To introduce oneself into a short story or a novel is, in my view, a great mistake. This would be a kind of autobiography, not fiction. 'A good novel tells us the truth about its hero but a bad novel tells us the truth about its author' (from *Heretics* by G.K. Chesterton). It is unsatisfactory (as well as potentially libellous) to represent people from real life. Fiction is imaginary; it may be sparked off by actual people and actual events but the author should be inventing characters and situations to illustrate his theme; when he creates the characters himself he understands their background, their motives and every turn of thought. How can we possibly know a real person in such depth? No one reveals his deepest secrets; there is always something he would never divulge to anyone. That 'something', known to you about your imaginary character, is often the mainspring of the story.

Your characters may, of course, be based on people you have met, probably an amalgam of many. They will almost certainly include aspects of yourself, the person you understand the best, but you will be creating an individual who has never existed before. What a challenge!

I love this quotation from Pirandello: 'When the characters are really alive before their author, the latter does nothing but follow them in their action, in their words, in the situation which they suggest to him' (from *Six Characters in Search of an Author*). If you write a novel you will probably find that the plot is suggested by the characters, almost as if they were acting out the story for themselves as the book progresses; it's like a film unrolling in front of your eyes. Sometimes the film breaks down and this is when your characters can help you out. Pay attention to their needs and they will restore the continuity.

Your main character should be someone for whom you, as the author, can feel affection. He may have faults and weaknesses but he should not, I think, be shallow or cowardly or cruel. There is a case for the anti-hero and we may sometimes enjoy reading about a villain to see if he gets his deserts, but in general the novice would be wise to choose a protagonist with whom he can readily sympathize.

If you are writing a who-dun-it, a thriller or a science-fiction story you may feel that plot and suspense are more important than the participants. In some ways this is true, but good characterization can only enhance any work of fiction and you would be well advised to study it carefully, whatever genre you eventually decide upon.

Choosing names

It is difficult to envisage a character until you have found the perfect name. Names are of great importance – nicknames, too – and you should never make do with something that does not satisfy you. Pansy O'Hara of Fountenoy Hall does not have the same ring as Scarlett O'Hara of Tara does it? Yet Margaret Mitchell started out with those names when she began to write *Gone With the Wind*. Somehow you will know if a name isn't quite right; listen to the inner voice and be guided by your intuition.

You may find inspiration on the internet especially if you need help with first names. There are websites which provide lists of the most popular names spanning a number of years and in various countries. This is useful if you are writing a story set in the recent past, for example the 1960s or 70s. The website www.babycentre.com provides the top ten US first names state by state for boys and girls. Another useful site is www.eponym.org which gives information on names in the UK and parts of Europe.

Be sure that your names are not too similar: for example, Claudia and Laura, Karen and Marion, Nigel and Simon. Contrast is important when you are choosing your cast. In the same way, make your forenames and surnames complement one another. Dominic Smith is good; Dominic Fotheringay is bad. Two flamboyant names together lack conviction. There's no harm in using the telephone book for ideas. Open a page at random and the gods may deliver the very surname you want.

How much description?

It was once customary to describe people in great detail; several pages were devoted to one character. Contemporary readers would seldom have the time or inclination to dally so long. They like to use their own imagination, building on the author's brief but telling phrases. Study this description of Cordelia in *An Unsuitable Job for a Woman* by P. D. James:

> Between their shoulders she could see her own reflection in the mirror above the bar. Today's face looked no different from yesterday's face; thick, light brown hair framing features which looked as if a giant had placed a hand on her head and the other under her chin and gently squeezed the face together; large eyes, browny-green under a deep fringe of hair; wide cheek bones; a gentle, childish mouth. A cat's face she thought, but calmly decorative among the reflection of coloured bottles and all the bright glitter of Mavis's bar.

You should also learn to weave your characterization into the development of the story as Ian McEwan has done in this extract from his brilliant novel, *The Cement Garden*:

> That night my parents argued over the bags of cement. My mother, who was a quiet sort of person, was furious. She wanted my father to send the whole lot back. We had just finished supper. While my mother talked my father used a penknife to scrape black shards from the bowl of his pipe on to the food he had barely touched. He knew how to use his pipe against her. She was telling him how little money we had and that Tom would soon be needing new clothes for starting at school. He replaced the pipe between his teeth like a missing section of his own anatomy and interrupted to say it was 'out of the question' sending the bags back and that was the end of it.

You will find that unusual detail is the most evocative. Everyone has some idiosyncrasy to distinguish him or her from the rest and you should search out these qualities in your characters. Look at this next example from H. E. Bates:

> Her mother sat upright in the rickshaw with something of the appearance of a moulting hawk: a woman of nearly sixty whose face had the arid shantung-yellow texture that came of thirty years' service under the Burma sun. She wore a dress of dull brown silk that, from the acid of much sweat, had gone completely to pieces under the arms. It had been

reprieved with parallelograms of lighter colour that would have shown badly if Mrs McNairn had ever lifted her arms more than waist high. In her determination to do no such thing she sat with her arms clenched in her lap, grasping the ivory handle of her white parasol. It was the parasol, with its hooked handle curving out from her clenched hands and knees, rather than anything in her angular beaky face, that gave the appearance of a faded bird of prey.

The Jacaranda Tree by H. E. Bates

It is usually more effective to portray a person at a particular time and place in the story, as with the last two examples, rather than give a more general description. At this point I would like to quote from an earlier book of mine called *The Craft of Novel-Writing* (Allison and Busby):

Sometimes a character becomes so real that he refuses to do what you have planned for him. When this happens, don't coerce him; it means you have created a real person with a will of his own and this is a marvellous moment in any novelist's life. Hold him on a light rein, as it were, giving him his head to a certain degree but ensuring that he does not stampede you out of your story. You must remain in command whilst allowing your creations to behave in accordance with the qualities you have given them. Write your scene with all the skill you have and let your instinct tell you whether or not it carries conviction. Creating imaginary characters is the core of novel-writing – and the possibilities are endless.

Character development

Bear in mind that your main character will undergo a change, subtle or violent, as a result of the various pressures he has faced. It may be the onset of bitterness or despair, a deepening of understanding, the effects – beneficial or otherwise – of falling in love, embracing some cause or belief, suffering an injury. In a short story the development of character is more difficult to express, but the novelist reveals the truth of his vision by the gradual change which takes place in his hero or heroine as the story unfolds; one of the signs of a 'cardboard' character is that he is exactly the same at the end of the book as he was at the beginning.

If the development is a change for the better, the novel will obviously be more satisfying to the reader, but there are no rules; you must write the way you feel, tell the truth for your characters, know them, and show them, and make the reader care about them.

Exercises in characterization

Getting into character

Some writers do a lot of preparatory work on characterization before writing a novel or even a short story. This may take the form of copious notes or experimental writing. This character 'research' should be looked on in the same light as an article writer looks upon research – it not only provides background information it also imparts the flavour of the subject.

Ultimately, thinking about your characters 'off the page', that is outside of the story itself, is the best preparation for writing there is, but here are a few suggestions which may help you, particularly if you are having trouble with a specific character.

1 **Write a passage or a scene in the first person** using the voice of the character in question. This 'monologue' will probably be entirely separate from the novel or story you are writing. Let your character speak. It could be on a mundane topic. This is not an exercise to develop plot but one to help you get under the skin of your character. The first person voice, of course, should be distinct from your own, completely different in fact. This exercise will help you to make that distinction.

2 **Fill in a job application** for your character, complete with CV, education history etc.

3 **Interview your character** either for an imaginary job or perhaps as a witness to some of the events in your story.

4 **Ask questions:** what makes this person laugh? When was the last time they cried? What is the character's most precious possession and why? What's the best thing they've ever done?

5 **Ask awkward questions:** Explore the things not immediately apparent on the surface. What do they think about lying? What was the last lie they told? What's the worst thing they've ever done?

6 **Travel with your character:** As you go through the routines of your non-writing day, put yourself in your character's shoes – how would he or she see the supermarket, etc.; react to the real life people and situations around you.

Exercise 13

Write a character study of 300 words minimum focussing on a living person. If you are a fiction-writer choose an imaginary person. Maximum 500 words.

Exercise 14

Write an imaginary correspondence between two of your favourite characters, either of your own creation or from literature. Make the letters quite short and restrict the overall number of words to 750.

Exercise 15

If you attempted Exercise 11, put your characters through the 'tests' outlined above making rough notes as you go along.

dialogue

In this chapter you will learn:
- the difference between real speech and dialogue
- how to present dialogue on the page
- how to ensure your dialogue relates to the story context.

'What is the use of a book,' thought Alice, 'without pictures and conversation?' We all know how she felt: the conversation you introduce into your fiction is of paramount importance. In this chapter we will consider the dialogue in short stories and novels. For stage or television dramas, where the characters are there in person, the approach is rather different, and radio drama demands a special technique of its own (see Chapters 17, Writing for Radio and 18, Stage and Screen).

Life versus art

No matter what type of fiction you are writing, the dialogue must sound as if real people are talking to each other, but fictional dialogue is very different from actual speech; the dull bits, the repetitions, the irrelevancies, must be pruned away, leaving a taut, interesting exchange which gives the *impression* of real speech.

A beginner once said to me, defending a page of tedious dialogue: 'But I heard two women saying all that in a bus shelter – I wrote it down in shorthand!' It's essential, of course, to listen (quite shamelessly) to conversations in queues and trains so that you are aware of the way in which many kinds of people speak to each other, but that is only background study. When you write the dialogue in your story you must be ruthless in cutting out every single word which does not carry the action forward or add something significant to the delineation of your characters. As you gain experience you will learn to incorporate both at the same time.

You might think you must make the dialogue boring if you are to portray a boring person. Not so. If you show the reaction of someone else, someone who is far from boring, your tedious character will be revealed effectively and yet you will keep the reader interested – and possibly amused as well. (If you find yourself putting two bores together, re-plan the scene!)

The following examples show how a beginner's story can be improved by editing. As you become more accomplished you will edit as you go along – or afterwards, depending on your personal preference.

> Marion was standing by the living room door with her coat on. 'I'll just have to pop down to the chemist's, John,' she explained. 'I've got to wash my hair tonight and I need some more shampoo. I didn't realize it was all used up and I can't

use soap because it makes my hair look dull, even if I rinse it over and over again. I won't be long – only about twenty minutes – unless there's a queue in the shop. When I get back we'll talk about that horrible letter you got from your father.'

'Right,' said John. 'I'll do a bit of weeding while you're out.'

Boring, isn't it? It sounds like a real conversation, but for fiction it needs a great deal of pruning.

Marion was standing by the living room door with her coat on. 'I'm just going down to the chemist's for some shampoo,' she said. 'When I get back we'll talk about that letter.'

If John is going to do a bit of weeding while she's out, we don't want to know about it; he needs to get up to something much more intriguing. And the details of the letter can be omitted because it's apparent that the reader is already in the picture.

Good dialogue consists of lively speeches, usually short, in which people interrupt one another, deceive one another, go off at a tangent, sometimes use bad grammar and strong language, but never ramble on about nothing of importance, as we do in real life. Everything your characters say must be right for *them*. A novice will sometimes make two people speak in exactly the same way, even using the same expressions.

'Bad' language

What about four-letter words? My own conviction is that we should allow our characters to use them (though not to excess) if it is appropriate for them to do so. An army sergeant would hardly say 'Go away!' if he found a man threatening his wife! If you dislike bad language this doesn't mean that you can't introduce it into your story; your characters will be doing plenty of things you disapprove of, besides swearing. But if you are so shocked by strong language that you can't write it (I once had a lady in my class who couldn't bring herself to say the word 'bloody' when she was reading out someone else's story) then you must choose the kind of characters who would not use the words you object to. My advice would be to write your dialogue truthfully (except in stories for children) but be prepared to bow to the editor's or publisher's wishes if he accepts your work and suggests amendments.

Dialect

Avoid dialect as far as possible; it's difficult to read. A Yorkshire miner must obviously sound like a Yorkshire miner but his speech should be expressed by the turn of phrase rather than by a swarm of apostrophes in place of letters. This will come easily if you are familiar with the kind of person you are writing about, and you should never choose to portray a section of the community which is not well known to you. You should be able to hear the rhythms and patterns of speech clearly and accurately in your mind.

He said, she said

It is sometimes suggested that writers should search for alternatives to 'he said' and 'she said' (he demanded, she wavered, he expostulated, etc.). This is not only unnecessary but inadvisable. Study the masters of prose such as Graham Greene, H. E. Bates and Iris Murdoch, and you will find that 'said' is used a great deal and does not intrude in the least unless you are particularly looking out for it. Alternatives, deliberately sought for by amateurs, intrude all the time. Here's an example:

'If Nicholas doesn't propose by the end of the month I shall ask him myself,' exclaimed Jean.

'Oh, Jean – you can't!' protested Susan.

'I can and I will,' affirmed Jean.

'If you do,' continued Susan, 'you'll lose him.'

'I agree,' averred Nigel ...

There are many occasions when no 'he said' is required, merely the speech itself, followed by the next one, but never allow confusion to arise by going on too long. If the reader has to count back to see who's saying what line your scene has failed.

Beware of the stilted phrase: 'I have told you that I did not do it' instead of 'I've told you I didn't do it.' Be sure to read your dialogue aloud; this is by far the best way to discover faults.

Dialogue in context

Novices often write their speeches in a vacuum. You should set your scene with great clarity so that we can picture your characters as they are speaking. I once had a student who wrote a marvellous exchange between two businessmen, wrangling for power. It was dramatic and well edited but it failed because there was no background for their confrontation. They began in a car, driving through a leafy, sun-dappled lane, but as the dialogue continued there was no more mention of the environment. After a page or two we forgot they were in a car and when at last they got out of it we were flabbergasted.

You can often indicate who is speaking by a verb of action rather than of speech, and this will help to give a visual image of the scene. For instance, ' "I think I'm going to cry." Myra turned her head away.' Or, 'Eric tapped out his pipe and put it in his pocket. "I've had enough – I'm going to bed." '

Dialogue layout

For layout of dialogue on the page, study good contemporary writing and note that a new paragraph is required each time a different character speaks. Action by a character who has just spoken or who is about to speak appears on the same line, as in the last two examples

Single inverted commas are usually employed for dialogue, with double ones for quotes within a speech (e.g. 'I saw "The Three Sisters" at our local theatre last week.') but publishers have their own preference and sometimes this procedure is reversed.

If thoughts are enclosed in inverted commas they can easily be confused with speech. My own technique is to begin the thought sequence with a capital letter: 'She thought, He's no idea what I'm driving at.' You might prefer a colon to a comma after 'She thought'.

Exercise 16

Write 500 words of dialogue in which two people engage in a violent quarrel. Set it out like a play, with only the two names, the words spoken and one line to set the scene, for example:
A woman and her teenage son in the kitchen.

setting

In this chapter you will learn:
- the role the setting should play in your story
- how to decide between real and imaginary settings
- how to develop a visual style.

Your choice of setting should be one of the first considerations and be closely related to the theme, characters and action. Think carefully before you decide and make certain that you have chosen the most telling location for every scene you plan.

You will probably be influenced by places you have known quite briefly, places which have remained in your memory. Before I wrote my third novel, *Kick a Tin Can,* we had been living for a short time at Taplow, in Berkshire. Our home was a tiny flat and I was so excited by the beautiful riverside mansions that I invented one, a composite of several I had seen, enhanced by imagination, as the main setting for the novel. It was the story of an affair between a rich married woman of 34 and a boy of 15 who lived in a slum.

> The Thames was quiet here, reflecting the dazzling facade of a large white house on the far bank. Wilfred imagined that a film star might live in such a place. There were conservatories, verandahs, a round tower with a shining gold weather-vane on the top, huge windows. A stone balustraded terrace, massed with pink geraniums, led to a long, well-kept lawn which sloped down to a landing stage and boathouse. The boathouse was empty, a cavern of mysterious green shadows and glimmers of refracted light. Beside it stood a weeping-willow tree and the lawn was surrounded by yews and cedars ranging back, thick and dark, behind the house itself, making its whiteness even more brilliant.

I wrote that many years ago and now I think it is too dense. The boathouse is essential because an important scene takes place there, but if I had the chance to rewrite it I would relinquish the conservatories and verandahs. Perhaps I would part with the tower as well, although I would hate to do so; I can still see that weather-vane glinting in the sunlight as clearly as if I were looking at a colour transparency. And later in the book:

> He looked around him with more than his usual disgust. What would Carol think, or Andrew, if they could see the place where he lived? It was nothing but a slum. Two rows of blackened little houses facing each other across a narrow cobbled street. Grimy lace curtains in the tiny windows with sometimes a dusty plant or a poor, miserable little budgie in a cage, to break the monotony. Old cigarette packets and torn newspapers in the gutters; dirty milk bottles in the doorways; the smell of stale fat; cats and children exploring

rubbish in an alley-way; women in curlers shouting at them... He saw a curtain twitch as he passed a window and caught the gleam of curious eyes on him.

The main fault in this extract, I think, is the repetition of the word 'in'. I created the two places, both imaginary but based on real life, to highlight the contrast between the main characters.

Real or imaginary setting?

A fictitious story may, of course, be set in an actual place, so long as it is sufficiently large and impersonal. You can set a novel in London, Chicago or Avignon, inventing street names, hotels and bars, but you would be well advised not to choose a small village which actually exists. You could hardly use the one and only hotel as a background for your drama; the manager might be very much put out, particularly if your story had a rather unsavoury theme! Small places, therefore, should be totally imaginary, but a rough idea of the location can be suggested by such phrases as 'hidden in a remote valley north of Lake Como' or 'just off the A33 between Winchester and Newbury'. Details of this kind give an illusion of reality but do not invite letters of complaint from your readers.

Developing a visual style

In Chapter 4, The Short Story and Chapter 9, Dialogue I have stressed the importance of seeing your background settings very clearly in your mind's eye. It is vital to picture your characters in a specific environment as they speak and move: the ability to see your story unreeling like a film is a skill you will need for fiction-writing and one which can be developed with practice if you have the basic gift.

Having captured your mental image, how are you to translate it into words? Study the following extract from a short story by Anton Chekhov entitled *Agafya*: 'Beyond the hill the sun was setting. All that was left of the sunset was a pale crimson shaft of light, and even that was beginning to be overspread with flecks of cloud, as burning coal might be with ashes.'

It's hard to believe, isn't it, that so striking a picture can be evoked by the use of such simple words and such a simple construction?

An unusual image sticks in the memory: the following scene from Margaret Drabble's *The Needle's Eye* will stay with me forever because the picture of the hen is so quaint and delightful.

> They were in a waste lot, a steep bombed site: the house that adjoined the bombsite had appropriated a small plot of land, doubtless unofficially, and had fenced it off with wire, and in it were these hens. The wall that fronted on to the site still showed vestiges of the bombed building that had stood there: the remains of a fireplace one storey up, a few scraps of wallpaper. In the fenced-off plot stood an armchair. In the armchair sat a feathery dusty old hen.

And how about this passage from *The French Lieutenant's Woman* by John Fowles, describing a woodland walk?

> It seemed strangely distinct, this undefiled dawn sun. It had almost a smell, as of warm stone, a sharp dust of photons streaming down through space. Each grassblade was pearled with vapour. On the slopes above his path the trunks of the ashes and sycamores, a honey gold in the oblique sunlight, erected their dewy green vaults of young leaves; there was something mysteriously religious about them, but of a religion before religion; a druid balm, a green sweetness over all …

I had to look up 'photons' (you too?) but that didn't matter because the writing is so pure and exquisite.

Colour, movement, light and shade are all-important when you visualize your scenes. You must know the time of the year, the quality of light in every room and street and garden you write about. You will not describe it all – how could you? – but you must be aware of it if you are to give the reader an acute sense of reality. Your characters should move in a setting which is as true to life as they are themselves. This is often overlooked. A novice will describe the sheen on a woman's hair, the colour and texture of her dress, but not her shadow on the wall as the sun streams through the window.

Your settings, of course, are not merely visual; we must hear the traffic, the footsteps, the birdsong; we must smell the appropriate smells – frying bacon, escaping gas, orange blossom, anaesthetic …

Write about what you know. Don't attempt to describe actual locations you have never visited or to invent imaginary ones with insufficient first-hand experience. You may argue that some writers get away with it after extensive research of travel books and brochures but I have always been against it. How can you hope to conjure up the elusive sounds and smells of a country you have never been to, or the particular atmosphere of an unknown town? I pride myself on a healthy imagination but I wouldn't dream of setting a book in Canada, for instance, until I had been there. I could do it superficially perhaps but there would be a myriad details I could never know about, and a native would recognize their absence at once. If you have never been to Venice, a football final, a bullfight, you would be unwise to write about them; books and films cannot provide you with sufficient atmosphere. Historical settings, of course, can only be brought to life on the basis of research and informed guesswork, but at least there is no one around to tell us we are wrong.

Describing imaginary places is one of the most satisfying aspects of a fiction-writer's job, so much so that he is apt to get carried away, introducing irrelevant details (like my conservatories and verandahs) and writing at too great a length. Limit yourself, in general, to no more than ten lines of description at a stretch, and make a habit of interspersing it with action.

> He pulled back the curtain a little and looked out into the November evening. Snow had begun to fall again in Ebury Street, large snow flakes moving densely, steadily, with visible silence, in the light of the street lamps, and crowding dimly above in the windless dark. A few cars hissed by, their sound muted and softened. The Count was about to say, 'It's snowing,' but checked himself. When someone is dying there is no point in telling him about the snow. There was no more weather for Guy.

> *(Nuns and Soldiers* by Iris Murdoch)

Have you ever read a better description of snowfall? Looking up from the page, I was surprised to see a summer's day.

Exercise 17
Choose a house, real or imaginary, and bring it vividly to life in not more than 200 words.

how to conduct an interview

In this chapter you will learn:
- how to prepare and plan for an interview
- how to conduct an interview
- how to turn your notes into copy.

I keep six honest serving-men
(They taught me all I knew);
Their names are What and Why and When
And How and Where and Who.

Rudyard Kipling

Interviewing is a skill and, as with any other, it's one which will
improve with practice. If you are an aspiring feature writer,
journalist, researcher, biographer or are writing your
autobiography, the ability to talk to people to gain further
information is invaluable. If you can then recall, select, write and
structure the relevant parts of the information you have gained
into a saleable piece of writing then you will be a successful writer.
Developing a good interview technique also marks your passage
into another phase in a writer's life – moving from your own
experiences to those of others. With this in mind, let's take a
closer look at this skill. We will divide the task into three parts:
before, during and after the interview.

Before the interview: preparation

Let's assume that you have discovered a person who has an
interesting job, lifestyle or past.

1 The first step is to make contact with the person concerned,
   asking if he or she would be willing to be interviewed and
   giving three or four possible dates. If you receive a favourable
   reply, write at once, thanking him for his kindness and
   mentioning the agreed date once again so he has a reminder.
2 Having got so far, telephone a day or two before the
   appointment to ask if he is agreeable to your using a tape-
   recorder. Some people hate to think that their every word is
   captured for replay, so don't be surprised if the answer is no. If
   your request is refused just accept it. It is very important to
   establish an easy relationship right from the start.
3 If the interviewee does agree to be taped, you should still be
   prepared to use only a notebook and pencil. Not only is there
   a possibility of the machine breaking down, but there is also
   the chance that your subject could have a change of heart at the
   last moment.
4 Arm yourself with a good notepad and pencils and if, like me,
   you know nothing of shorthand, put in some practice at
   writing very quickly in your own abbreviated longhand.

5 Arrange a mock interview with a friend, jotting down answers with all possible speed and making sure that you can decipher your scribble afterwards. Use only half the page available before starting a fresh page. This enables you to fill out the notes and make further observations later.

6 Do your 'homework' thoroughly. Read everything you can about the subject and plan your questions carefully. Twelve is a good number. If you are venturing outside your own field of knowledge familiarize yourself with the jargon of the subject so that you are not frequently interrupting the interviewee's 'flow' by querying terminology once the interview is underway.

7 When planning consider what questions your reader would want asked. Arrange them in a logical order, paying special attention to the first one, which should be designed to put the interviewee at his ease. However, do not feel that you must stick slavishly to this plan, you may discover more by straying a little off the beaten track. Having made a plan at least you will know where the beaten track is and can get back to it later!

During the interview

1 Don't arrive late – nor yet too early.

2 Be confident. Assume a relaxed and confident manner even though you may feel that you are far more nervous than he is. *Never* apologize for your inexperience or belittle yourself in any way.

3 If you use a tape-recorder, test it out just before you start; and use a new tape and batteries.

4 Whatever answers you receive to your questions, do not be drawn into an argument. You are there to talk about *him* and *his* views, not your own, and you should in fact say very little. The interview will probably not be of the investigative kind, there will be little or no sub-text – just an enthusiastic interest in someone else's subject.

5 Don't make the mistake of being so eager to get to the next question that you forget to listen to answer to the last one! It sounds like a beginner's mistake but you have only to listen to some below par radio and television interviews to hear it in action!

6 Don't stay too long. No matter how well things are going, an hour-and-a-half is probably about right. I must admit that I enjoy being interviewed but some people dislike it. You will soon see which are which and conduct your interview accordingly.

After the interview

If you take notes, whether in shorthand or longhand, you would be wise to write them out in detail the very moment you get home. You will then recall additional points you couldn't get down on paper. Writing up a piece from pages of notes is a demanding task at the best of times, but your work will be very much easier if you expand your jottings while the encounter is fresh in your memory.

Writing the piece

When you quote an interviewee directly in the article you are representing what the person actually meant rather than giving a verbatim quote. You will use only some of the words the person used to convey the essence of what they said. Even if you did use a tape-recorder and could quote verbatim – it would still be necessary for you to edit what the person actually said. The rules of dialogue apply just as much to non-fiction as fiction – the boring bits have to be taken out!

Interspersing quotes in the narrative of the article breaks the piece up and helps to bring the subject to life. Your subject will very much appreciate the opportunity to check the typescript for errors before you offer it for publication. You might have made a factual mistake or misspelt a proper name. Tell him you will send him a copy, and explain that it must be returned to you at once or there will not be time for you to amend it.

Other types of interview

Not all interviews are face to face. Sometimes, if the subject is agreeable, an interview can be conducted over the phone. Email interviews are possible, again if the subject is agreeable, either one question at a time or with the questions being emailed in advance.

The internet makes it possible for private chat rooms to be arranged and video for conferencing. These developments may get the job done and allow some interviews to happen which would otherwise have been impossible because of distance, etc., but I doubt if the face-to-face method will ever be bettered – after all, it is said that 65 per cent of all communication is non-verbal.

Exercise 18

Choose a friend who is willing to be the subject of a practice interview and prepare 12 suitable questions on a particular aspect of their lives or an important event.

Exercise 19

Look at a number of feature articles in different magazines and note how the writers used quotes in the piece. Some of the factual information will have been included in the narrative of the article and some in quotes. Draw up an imaginary list of interview questions which you think the author would have needed to ask.

12 revision with style

In this chapter you will learn:
- how to revise and edit your work
- how to enable your true writing style to shine through
- the importance of good grammar and punctuation.

The craft of revision

Revision, or editing, gives you the opportunity to see the bigger picture and to evaluate, scene by scene in a story, section by section in a non-fiction piece of writing, the contribution each makes to the overall work. If a scene proves to be irrelevant it must go even if it does include favourite phrases and sentences.

It is one of the most important aspects a writer has to learn. When the beginner thinks a piece of work is finished, that's when the hard work begins. A daunting thought, perhaps, but you will find that every sentence you write requires more consideration than you ever anticipated.

Here is an example of the way in which I battled with a sentence to make it more concise, more telling. I was describing a night journey by train:

(a) Lighted stations flung themselves for an instant against the window and then were sucked away into the blackness.

(b) Small lighted stations flared against the window from time to time and then were sucked into the blackness.

(c) Little lighted stations flared against the window from time to time and were instantly sucked into the blackness.

(d) Little stations flared against the window from time to time and were instantly sucked away into the darkness.

Perhaps you are thinking that one can go on too long with such amendments, draining the life from your prose. There is always the danger of over-correction but the novice is much more likely to err the other way, and in any case the practice of improvement is an essential part of your training as a writer.

Don't you agree, in version (c), that 'lighted' is unnecessary? The station would hardly 'flare' if it were not lighted! And 'darkness', following 'into the', has a smoother sound than 'blackness'. Euphony is of great importance; that's why you should always read your work aloud, preferably on to a tape-recorder so that you can check the manuscript as you listen to the playback. My final preference was for (d).

Working preferences

Once you are sure that a scene deserves its place in the piece as a whole ensure that each sentence within the scene can justify its existence.

Some writers feel the need to perfect each sentence as far as possible before going on to the next; I work that way myself. Others prefer to rough the whole thing out in full and then go back to revise it. In any case, your work will be subject to constant revision right to the final draft, so don't be discouraged if you have to cross things out and scribble alterations between the lines and up the sides and on spare bits of paper. My working pages are still festooned with arrows and asterisks, and as soon as I have typed out a fair copy from my longhand muddle, I find myself scrawling amendments all over it again. Take a look at my last corrected draft of the Introduction to this book (see next page).

Computer users will probably be laughing at my method of revision, but writers are individualists and we must all choose the best way of achieving our aims. It may seem that the computer is the answer to everything because you can continually edit your work as you go but this, too, requires discipline if you are to avoid the temptation of spending more time revising than writing.

Points for revision

The following pointers will help you to analyse your early drafts and amend them constructively. You should refer to these when revising your work on the exercises set so far.

1 Have you begun in the right place?
We have already seen the importance of the opening passages in earlier chapters and this applies in all types of writing – fiction, non-fiction, poetry or drama. Always ask: Is this the best moment to engage the reader in the substance of what I want to say?

2 Are there any unintentional repetitions?
Inadvertent repetition is always a danger. When you are writing in the heat of inspiration you will probably repeat yourself; this is normal and natural. The secret is to revise later with care, eliminating every word which could reduce the readability of your prose. The reader wants every sentence to be new and fresh, otherwise he or she will be thinking – perhaps subconsciously – I've heard that before – that's boring!'

Repetition can be used deliberately for a specific reason, for example, to emphasize, underline a point or even jolt the reader. Take this example from *The War Lover* by John Hersey:

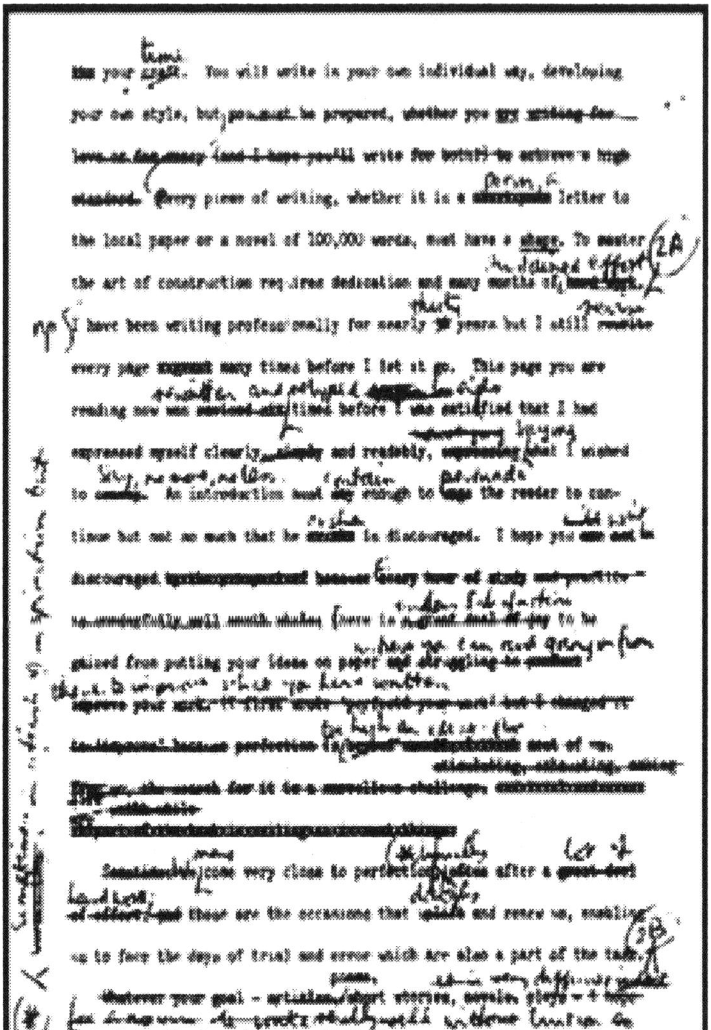

final draft of part of my introduction, before retyping

Each of Buzz's landings was an experiment, a delicate search for a new and better way to find that breathtaking split moment when all those tons of metal ceased being carried by the wind and were accepted back by the mother ground. He held the wheel of the column in his fingertips and seemed to be feeling, with the sensitivity of a blind man reading Braille, for the very very very end of flight.

Three verys in a row would normally be considered clumsy but in this instance I think they have been used with extraordinary courage and artistry.

The inadvertent repetition of words and phrases is one thing but a subtler problem may be the repetition of ideas. Perhaps, without realizing it, you have said the same thing twice, in different ways.

3 Have you strayed from your theme?
The next hazard is irrelevance. Have you included any material which is not directly related to the central theme? You may be tempted to put in details which are of personal significance but which have little or no relevance to the subject. Edit them out (however much it hurts!) and you will see a great improvement.

4 Are all of your descriptions relevant?
Watch out for long descriptions. You may be describing a place or a person at too great a length. You can easily be carried away by your own exuberance when you care deeply about your subject. This may not be a bad thing, *provided that you edit it later*.

5 Is your research invisible?
When you need more information for your work in progress, fiction or non-fiction, you will probably unearth all manner of fascinating details connected with your subject. The internet, the local library, talking to people with specialist knowledge may have played a part in your researches. It can be a temptation to include too much research in your final manuscript. Many of the facts you have discovered might seem so beguiling that you cannot bear to part with them. Be strong! You will ruin your work if you weight it down with unnecessary detail. Sort out the most relevant and file the rest away for later reference.

So, be selective when you revise. Cutting demands discrimination and courage but the rewards are great.

6 Strong opinions
We all have our views on religion, politics, philosophy, etc. Some of us have very strong opinions indeed. But unless you are writing

a non-fiction book or an article on a specific subject which you are well qualified to discuss, you should not allow your personal views to colour your prose. Fiction should, I believe, be completely free of moralizing. Never try to convert your reader to your ways of thinking, in however succinct a manner. In one of my early novels I made this mistake and had to rewrite several chapters when I saw how wrong I had been.

You can, of course, allow one of your characters to voice your own opinions, but in that case be sure to let another character state an opposing opinion. This makes for good dialogue and entertaining conflict. Your own attitudes will probably seep into your story between the lines but you should not deliberately try to influence the reader. Nobody likes to be preached at.

This advice may be difficult to accept. As writers, we need to communicate, and especially we want to express our deep convictions about the human situation. Nevertheless, this is an area of expression which we must deal with very carefully if we are to engage and entertain our reader.

7 The dead wood stage

Most of us can take any page of our work and improve it immensely by the removal of what I call 'dead wood'. These are words or phrases which are unnecessary, adding nothing but tedium. Here are some examples, with the 'dead wood' in italics: She crossed *over to the other side of* the road; they shared the *same* taxi; it was the first time they had *ever* quarrelled; he was *quite* sure that she meant to insult him.

The following is an extract from an article written by Richard Curtis, and called *Four Rules and a Suggestion*. It appeared in the Observer newspaper in 1994 and then in the book *Four Weddings and a Funeral, The Screenplay*, published by Corgi Books. If you think talented, gifted professionals write one draft and then wait for the world's applause, read what Richard Curtis has to say:

Rule Four is – don't count the rewrites or it will drive you mad.

These were the rewrites on 'Four Weddings' – five for Emma before it was ever handed in. One after talking to Duncan, my producer and Debra at Working Title, the production company. Then two big ones for Mike Newell, the director, and Duncan, as we tried to give every character proper stories, rather than just jokes. Then there was one after the first round of casting: actors reading the lines tend to show just how clunky the script is! The next rewrite came after

Channel 4 expressed worries about it all being a bit 'smart'. Then the film was delayed for six months, then there was one long rewrite to fill the time and to try to crack the really knotty problems with the end. At one point Emma and I escaped to Europe, and spent a month on one 2 minute scene. Then there was another rewrite during the second round of casting. Then one when the budget went from £3.5 million to £3.2. Then another one when it went from £3.2 million to £2.7, which consisted of cutting down the cast: 'a' vicar, became 'the vicar you saw earlier'. After the read through (when no-one laughed at 15% of the 'jokes' and DID laugh at 25% of the serious bits), there was another hefty hack. During rehearsals another. That's seventeen, and I've got a nasty feeling I've forgotten one or two. And the horrible thing about this rule is part two of it – don't resent the rewrites – the awful painful truth is that the script probably did get a bit better each time.

A final word of advice on revision: when you think you have finished, put your manuscript away for a few days and then read it again with a fresh eye. A few days' break might just do the trick.

The art of good style

It may seem that the pruning you have to do as a beginner will remove all trace of individuality from your work, leaving only a skeleton of that original concept which excited you so much. Don't be discouraged; one of the greatest problems any writer has to overcome is that of preserving spontaneity whilst honing away irrelevancies, repetitions and clumsy phrases. It can be done and it has to be done. Just give yourself time. Remember, pruning away the clutter will reveal your style not inhibit it. Where would the rose be without pruning?

The mastery of good style

When a writer is highly talented but lacks experience he or she is often tempted to use flowery language and over-complicated phraseology. The love of words and the facility which talent engenders can destroy the *clarity and simplicity* which (as Stendhal noted) is the essence of good style.

If you write in your own way you will gradually establish an individual style without conscious effort. I have been impressed, during many years of teaching creative writing, by the amazing variety in the work produced by complete beginners, unique, unmistakable and individual.

Study excellence

Although you should not attempt to copy anyone else's style, you can certainly learn from the writers you admire, study how they achieve their effects, and try to eliminate your own faults accordingly. For instance, in Chapter 9, Dialogue I pointed out that H. E. Bates used 'he said' and 'she said' far more than might be expected. This approach can be emulated without copying his style. Two of my favourite writers are Lawrence Durrell and Graham Greene. Their styles, as you may know, are totally different and I have learned from both and been inspired by them whilst in no way trying to mould my writing on theirs. Lawrence Durrell, with his ornate literary turn of phrase, has been accused of verbosity and this criticism might be justified if he were a lesser writer. Being the master he is, he can get away with it. Perhaps, in the course of time, you too might 'get away with it' but in the early stages I would suggest that you write clearly and simply, taking inspiration from Graham Greene rather than Lawrence Durrell. Wordy prose, over-complex and over-poetic, is certainly to be avoided. In a beginner this very fault may indicate a writer of great potential, but he must learn his trade and bear in mind that a direct contemporary style will find greater favour with editors and publishers.

The enemies of good style

Clichés

A cliché is a phrase, probably once apt and fresh, which has become stale and unimaginative through overuse. Examples include: 'at the end of the day', 'the bottom line', 'when the chips are down', 'over the moon', 'weak at the knees', 'white as a sheet'. But it doesn't stop with everyday phrases. In *The New Fowler's Modern English Usage* we're reminded that 'in the course of the 20C. the word cliché has come to be applied to commonplace things of other kinds – visual images, stock situations, remarks in radio and TV plays (and now if you'll excuse me I've got work to do), ideas, attitudes etc.'

Beware, too, those cliché situations: the woman who drops a glass when she hears some bad news; the husband who arrives home unexpectedly to find his wife in the arms of another man; the suicide note on the mantelpiece. Good style has a lot to do with freshness of vision.

Sentimentality

There is a world of difference between sentimentality and sentiment. Sentiment is sincere emotion – compassion, sorrow, love, delight. Sentimentality is mawkish over indulgence in emotion for effect. Your own good taste will tell you the difference, but the distinction can sometimes be a tricky one.

When you feel very deeply about a character or a situation, you can spoil a moving scene without realizing it. You need to be particularly self-critical in such cases and the advice of a trusted friend could be helpful.

Clumsy phrases

The euphony of the sentence, that is, the pleasant sound it should have, has a strong bearing on style. The writing may be correct grammatically but have a hard, jerky sound, leaving the reader with a sense of irritation rather than pleasure. For instance, 'every room and garden and street' is less harmonious than 'every room and street and garden'. Reading aloud will help, and if you stumble over a phrase, this may indicate that it needs revision. Your writing should run smoothly and easily, except on the rare occasions when you might choose an eccentric construction to obtain a certain effect.

Be wary of adjectives

Most beginners love adjectives. It was years before I really understood that, far from enhancing descriptions, they can have a deadening effect. In order to point this out to my students I ask them to write a descriptive piece of 300 words *without the use of a single adjective*. It isn't easy but the results are an unfailing delight; some of the exercises are the best work the students have produced to date. When the pieces are finished, one adjective may be added, and the indulgence of this luxury makes it clear to everyone that adjectives should be chosen with infinite care.

The following 'no adjectives' exercise was written by a beginner in one of my classes. I quote it to allay your natural resistance to such a formidable task.

The Homecoming by Dorothy Wright

She turned the key in the lock, the door swung open and she stepped into the hall. Sunlight followed her in. She flicked the curtains at the window farther apart, and another shaft of light spread into the room. A mirror picked up the radiance, dust danced wherever the sun caught it.

The stairs stretched upwards on the left. She knew exactly what was in the cupboard underneath them – the vacuum cleaner, an assortment of boxes and a row of hooks bulging with coats. She recognised the ornaments on the shelf fixed over the radiator, the presents she and the others had brought back from holidays in Cornwall or on the Continent. Even the pictures greeted her like friends from childhood. The ticking of the clock standing in the corner caught her attention, and she saw that in ten minutes it would strike four o'clock.

But it was the table that drew her right inside. It stood in its place against the wall, the top shining from years of polishing. Its legs, and the stretchers joining them near their base, showing signs of maltreatment and damage in the past, but the carving on the drawer was as she remembered.

Two candlesticks stood on it, their metal twinkling. Between them on a mat was a bowl of flowers wearing fragrance like a halo. She moved closer, dropped her suitcase, and traced the carving on the drawer with her fingers, gently, lovingly, almost reverently. Then she leaned forward. With one hand she cupped a bloom and inhaled its sweetness. With the other she caressed the patina of the tabletop. It seemed to hold the warmth of life, and to welcome her home.

For her one luxury adjective, the author chose the word 'delicate': 'the carving on the drawer was as delicate as she remembered.' (You may be thinking that 'bulging', 'shining' and 'twinkling' are used as adjectives, but for the purpose of this exercise we mustn't be too pedantic.) The important thing is to aim high: trying for a difficult target usually produces quality, even if one falls a little short. In an exercise where adjectives are forbidden, the author will make compensatory use of adverbs. This adds liveliness to the piece but of course one must beware of using too many.

Once you have developed a good natural style you will never lose it. It will be there at your fingertips – a lasting pleasure for yourself and for those who read your work.

Incorrect grammar

Small slips of grammar can be corrected by an editor or publisher but serious faults will spoil your chances of success. If you feel inadequate in these respects you should take a course, or work through the exercises in books such as *Teach Yourself English Grammar*.

Bad spelling is a much less serious problem than bad grammar which can wreck whole paragraphs. You can check your spelling with a dictionary or use the computer's spell checker although, remember, a correctly spelt word used in the wrong context is invisible to the computer. Do I hear you say, 'My computer has a grammar checker so I'm well looked after'? To a degree, perhaps, but computer grammar checkers have a long way to go before their 'suggestions' can be followed with confidence. There is still no substitute for individual study and there probably never will be.

Punctuation

It is outside the scope of this book to discuss punctuation in detail but I would urge you to study in particular the use of colons and semicolons and to limit the use of the exclamation mark; my own letters to friends are peppered with them but I have learned to restrict their use to the minimum in my novels.

Punctuation is very important, but some new writers are under the impression that the editor will correct it if it's wrong. Not so. If you don't understand the proper use of the semicolon, for instance, your writing will lack the authenticity of the professional. Many beginners don't really know when to use a semicolon and this can mean that they avoid it altogether. The semicolon is a gift to any writer.

According to the *New Shorter Oxford Dictionary* a semicolon is 'A punctuation mark consisting of a dot placed above a comma (;), indicating a discontinuity of grammatical construction greater than that indicated by a comma but less than that indicated by a full stop.'

Here are two examples:

'He knew there was no escape; the door was already locked.'

'The plants most likely to succeed in sandy soils are those which like sharp drainage; frequently they are sun-lovers.'

The second phrase often expands the original statement. Reading your work aloud will help you to decide whether you need a comma, a semicolon or a full stop. Colons, dashes, brackets and exclamation marks also demand careful consideration. Most new writers use far too many exclamation marks.

Many of us were taught that every sentence must contain a verb, that we must never begin a sentence with 'And' or end one with a preposition and so on. I suppose it was good basic training but it hampers some of my creative writing students. A sentence without a verb may puzzle you, but see how effective they can be: 'An empty room. No sound but a bluebottle at the window.'

If you are shaky on grammar or punctuation do take the trouble to study them in depth; then you can feel secure in your ability to express yourself clearly and correctly.

Exercise 20

Write a descriptive piece of 300 words or so, using no adjectives. When the work is finished, add one only.

Exercise 21

Imagine: an editor has just phoned you saying he would be delighted to accept your 1000 word story/article but first you must cut it by 125 words. With this in mind, take a completed piece of your work and see what 'savings' could be made without affecting the piece as a whole.

finding titles

In this chapter you will learn:
- the differing roles titles play in fiction and non-fiction
- the current trends in children's titles
- how copyright affects titles.

Although a title may be the last thing you think of, it will be the first thing the editor (and hopefully the reader) will see, so it's worth spending time and effort on this important element. Even if you have known what the title should be right from the first draft you should still give alternative titles due consideration.

Some titles are easy to find, especially those for non-fiction books which require only a plain statement of the subject *Cooking for One*; *The Private Life of Plants*; *Make Your Own Classical Guitar*; *Teach Yourself Creative Writing*.

As Gordon Wells says in *How To Write Non-Fiction Books* (Writers' Bookshop): 'Notice the use, in technical titles, of such phrases as 'How to ...', 'Successful ...', and 'Profit from ...' They all suggest that buying the book will benefit the reader. Notice too that 'technical' titles clearly indicate the subject.' Titles for articles and short stories also need care.

Articles

Define the job you want your title to do. Inform? Amuse? Intrigue? The answer will depend on the type of article you are writing and the publication you are aiming for. Your market research will have told you the style and length of titles most suitable for your chosen market.

Informative titles tell the reader directly what to expect if they read on, for example, *Lazy Gardening*; *Herbs for Your Windowsill*; *Revamp Your Living Room*; *21 Ways to Simplify Your Finances*.

Humorous titles can be informative too: *Acupuncture – What's the Point?*; *Eat Fat, Get Slim*; *How to Find Another Husband, (Inside of the One You've Got)*.

Short stories

Short story titles often do more than just inform or amuse. A good title can mean one thing to the reader at the outset but take on an altogether different meaning once the story has been read, for example, *A Dog's Chance* has two quite different meanings, it's literal one plus a more colloquial one implying having little or no chance at all. If both meanings are utilized by the plot then what is quite an ordinary title works well for that story. The clue to a twist ending story is often 'hidden' in the title.

Exercise 22
Can you think of other well-known phrases which could be taken two ways? If so, jot them down and think how a plot might be woven from those meanings.

Editors, I'm afraid, will sometimes change your title without consulting you; this is one of the irritations we have to accept. You may, in some cases, prefer the new title, but if you don't there's nothing much you can do. You probably won't even know about it until the magazine is on the bookstalls!

The novel

The title of a novel is quite a different matter. It makes a stronger impact on the reader than a short-story title and it will certainly not be changed without your agreement. It's important to find one which is arresting, unusual and perfectly in tune with the book. Sometimes the title comes first, expressing your theme and sparking off a whole novel. The perfect word or phrase will suddenly flash into your mind, straight from heaven, so that you cry out, 'Yes – that's it!' More often, however, the book is complete except for the title and you can think of nothing that pleases you.

Key words, I think, might help. Write down as many words as you can think of which relate to your novel – the theme, the main characters, the setting, the climax – and juggle them around until something promising occurs to you. Failing that, look up your key words in a dictionary of quotations or *Roget's Thesaurus* and see if you come across something appropriate. Don't be tempted to use a quotation, however, unless it really fits. And be sure that the title you choose is right for the mood of your story.

The notion of paradox can inspire an attractive title: *A Bouquet of Barbed Wire*; *Nuns and Soldiers*; *A Raging Calm*.

One-word titles can be strong and effective: *End-game*; *Airport*; *Birdsong*; *Splitting*. One-word titles with the definite article have produced a wealth of excellent titles: *The Bell*; *The Hippopotamus*; *The Information*.

Many novelists find names for their books in a phrase which describes the main character: *The French Lieutenant's Woman*; *Our Man in Havana*; *The Rector's Wife*; *The Ragman's*

Daughter; *The Dreamthief's Daughter*; *The Bonesetter's Daughter*. Longer titles can also be fascinating: *The Loneliness of the Long Distance Runner*; *The Five Quarters of the Orange*; *A Second Chance at Eden* but remember they can be difficult to fit onto the spine of the book, particularly if your name is also a long one.

Some titles are mysterious or ambiguous making the reader notice the title and think about it further, for example, *Sushi for Beginners* stands out in a row of novels as if the book has been misfiled as does *How To Be Good*. *The Edible Woman* has a shock element, so too does *The Blind Assassin*, (both the latter titles by Margaret Atwood).

Children's titles

These need to be both descriptive and distinctive. Flicking through a publisher's catalogue or browsing the children's section of your local bookshop will give you the flavour of what's in vogue. Here are a few examples divided into age categories.

0–5 years:
The Very Hungry Caterpillar; *The Lion Who Wanted to Love*; *The Gruffalo*; *Harry and the Bucketful of Dinosaurs*; *Hairy Maclary from Donaldson's Dairy*; *Six Dinner Sid*; *The Tiger Who Came to Tea*; *I Will Not Ever Never Eat a Tomato*; *Where the Wild Things Are*; *Rusty's Bone*; *That's Not My Puppy…*; *Duck in the Truck*. Six words seems to be a maximum.

5–8 years
The Killer Underpants; *A Handful of Horrid Henry*; *The Owl Who Was Afraid of the Dark*; *The Twits*; *The Hundred Mile An Hour Dog*; *The Hodgeheg*.

8–12 years
Harry Potter and the Philosopher's Stone; *Artemis Fowl*; *The Toilet of Doom*; *Goodnight Mister Tom*; *Shadow of the Minotaur*; *The Illustrated Mum*; *The Kite Rider*; *Losing the Plot*.

Teens/young adult
Skellig; *I Capture the Castle*; *Feeling Sorry for Celia*; *Junk*; *Noughts and Crosses*; *Raspberries on the Yangtze*; *Holes*; *Refugee Boy*.

My own most successful book was a novel for young adults called *Escape on Monday*. I suppose we all want to escape from something – and specially on a Monday! That title took a lot of finding but it was well worth the effort.

Copyright

There is no copyright in titles but it is in your own interest, as well as that of the other author, to avoid duplication. 'How does one find out what's been used before?' you may ask. Bearing in mind that there are thousands of new books published every year, it would be well-nigh impossible to keep track of all those in print, never mind the ones which are out of print but still in the libraries. However, to get an indication whether or not a title is currently available try the search facilities of a few of the internet book shops. The search of over one and a half million different titles will take only a matter of seconds. Try www.amazon.co.uk; www.amazon.com; www.bol.com or any of the major booksellers – they all have their own websites.

Exercise 23
Choose alternative titles for any three well-known novels.

Exercise 24
Take a notebook and pen to your local bookshop. Make a note of six titles which interest you without actually looking at the cover, blurb, etc. Take a moment or two to decide what it was about the title which attracted you. Then allow yourself to look at the book. Take care, this could prove to be an expensive exercise!

part three

avenues and directions

writing poetry

In this chapter you will learn:
- how to experiment with poetry to develop your creativity
- the role of construction in poetry
- how to submit poetry for publication.

'There's no money in poetry,' someone complained to Robert Graves. 'No,' he replied, 'and there's no poetry in money!' It is by no means easy to sell a poem, but fortunately the need to express oneself in verse is usually an artistic and emotional need rather than a financial one. Children write poems for love alone and many adults do the same. People who contemplate the beauty of nature, long for freedom, worship God, or love one another in any of a thousand different ways, will often find they can express their feelings in poetry.

Poetry and creativity

A little 'creative doodling' can help to get you in the mood for a writing session. The nudging of words into sentences simply because you like the sound of them in your head or the look of them on the page can open up the creative pathway leading onward to that day's writing.

If you are between projects and looking for a new direction, exploring the poetic landscape is a great 'loosener' of ideas and themes. This kind of exercise can be very rewarding. The freedom of not knowing what you will write next, or where it came from, is often intriguing and stimulating.

Developing your interest in poetry

You will find it instructive to read the classics of poetry, old and new, and to study the imagery, the metre, the rhyme schemes, the overall design. If you want to specialize in poetry you should read *The Craft of Writing Poetry* by Alison Chisholm, an excellent and comprehensive guide published by Allison and Busby. Poetry magazines, including *The Poetry Review*, published quarterly, are listed in *The Writer's Handbook* and *The Writers' and Artists' Yearbook*. Both books give further information of interest to aspiring poets.

The Poetry Society (established 1909) has an excellent and extensive website (www.poetrysoc.org.uk) which includes advice, details of competitions, meetings and events. You can read the current winners of the National Poetry Competition plus those commended by the judges, as well as a comprehensive list of links to other interesting and useful websites well worth exploring. You can also contact *The Poetry Society* at 22 Betterton Street,

London WC2H 9BX. You will find more useful websites listed under the Poetry section of Chapter 22, Research and the Internet, References and Resources.

Being self-critical

How can you tell if your poems are good, bad or indifferent? That is a question I hesitate to answer. When we reflect that the work of some of the most distinguished contemporary poets is considered by some critics to be meaningless, we can understand how difficult it is to assess the true value of any poem. But there is, as always, a need for self-criticism. Re-writing, editing and refining are essential parts of the process, searching out clichés, the banal, forced rhymes and temporary deviations from the rhythm of the poem. These are all beginners' faults which can be corrected with work and patience.

Poems sometimes develop gradually, evolving through a number of drafts until you find that you have reached the version which is right. This might be the appropriate time to offer it to the outside world for criticism. If you are a member of a writers' group you should be able to get a reaction from its members, paying special attention to the comments of those who specialize in poetry either as writers or readers. Later, if you have decided that this is the branch of creative writing for you, you might consider the Poetry Prescription service offered to members of *The Poetry Society*. There is a fee but in return your work will receive 'an honest and rigorous response' from an established poet. But remember it is best not to seek criticism before you are ready for it.

Appreciating poetry

Poetry is such a personal thing; if it delights us, moves us deeply or opens new windows on life, then *for us* it has succeeded. Here are some lines from modern poets which have remained in my memory. Why not keep a notebook for your own selection?

This lawn graced with the candle-flames of crocus
From *A Happy View* by Cecil Day Lewis

There is a pike in the lake
whose blue teeth eat the midnight stars
From *Juniper Holds to the Moon* by Laurie Lee

The force that drives the water through the rocks
Drives my red blood
From *The Force that Through the Green
Fuse Drives the Flower* by Dylan Thomas

The night sky is only a sort of carbon paper,
Blueblack, with much-poked periods of stars
Letting in the light, peephole after peephole –
A bonewhite light, like death, behind all things.
From *Insomniac* by Sylvia Plath

Take a black length of water, leave it rippling as the day dies,
By morning it will be stretched taut, pale and motionless, stiff silk.
From *Cold Spell* by Vernon Scannell

What passing-bells for these who die as cattle?
Only the monstrous anger of the guns
From *Anthem for Doomed Youth* by Wilfred Owen

Construction

There is no better training than to compose a sonnet. The
discipline of a set format is extremely valuable, whatever kind of
verse you eventually choose to write.

Then hate me when thou wilt: if ever, now;
Now while the world is bent my deeds to cross,
Join with the spite of fortune, make me bow,
And do not drop in for an after-loss:
Ah, do not, when my heart hath scap'd this sorrow,
Come in the rearward of a conquer'd woe;
Give not a windy night a rainy morrow,
To linger out a purpos'd overthrow.
If thou wilt leave me, do not leave me last,
When other petty griefs have done their spite,
But in the onset come: so shall I taste
At first the very worst of fortune's might.

And other strains of woe, which now seem woe,
Compar'd with loss of thee, will seem not so.
Sonnet Number XC by William Shakespeare

You will find that the best poems have a single theme – the
inspirational idea – and that this central theme is expressed in a
form which also has unity. Shakespeare's sonnets are prime
examples. The structure, as you will see, comprises fourteen lines,

the rhyme scheme being abab/cdcd/efef/gg. Each line has ten syllables, with the stress on the second syllable of each pair: Then *hate/* me *when/* thou *wilt*: if *ev/* er, *now*. This is known as *iambic pentameter* and Shakespeare's plays are written mostly in this form: 'Once *more/* unto/ the *breach*, dear *friends,/* once *more*'; 'The /qual/ity/ of *mer*/cy *is/* not *strain'd'*.

You have no need to bother about the theory unless you want to. 'Poetry is the language in which man explores his own amazement,' said Christopher Fry. You can do that just as well if you have never heard of iambic pentameter!

The following poem has always been one of my special favourites. Study the imagery, rich and dense, in keeping with the subject, and the unusual rhyme scheme.

> Glory be to God for dappled things –
> For skies of couple-colour as a brinded cow;
> For rose-moles all in stipple upon trout that swim;
> Fresh-firecoal chestnut-falls; finches' wings:
> Landscape plotted and pieced – fold, fallow, and plough;
> And all trades, their gear and tackle and trim.
>
> All things counter, original, spare, strange;
> Whatever is fickle, freckled (who knows how?)
> With swift, slow; sweet; sour; adazzle, dim;
> He fathers-forth whose beauty is past change:
> Praise him.
>
> *Pied Beauty* by Gerard Manley Hopkins

Fixed verse forms

The sonnet is one of the most well known fixed verse forms but there are many more which you might like to study and try your hand at, for example, the rondeau, the villanelle and the sestina are among them. The limerick is another fixed verse form, probably the most famous of all – or infamous!

If you would like to discover more about fixed verse forms visit the Google website at www.google.co.uk and click on the *Web Directory* section at the top of the page. Next click on *Arts* and then *Literature* and you will see listed an amazing array of topics including *Poetry*. Explore and enjoy!

You may prefer to discard conventional patterns – the choice between a traditional or a free form is a matter of personal taste – but some kind of shape is required no matter how unorthodox your verse may be.

The Haiku

If you are not quite ready for the fixed verse forms at this stage, why not try the simple and delightful Haiku? This is a poem of three lines which captures a fleeting image, a sense of beauty, wonder or sadness. It is based on a Japanese form developed in the seventeenth century and typified by the poet Basho (1643–94). The Haiku (plural Haiku), in the original Japanese, was a poem of 17 syllables (5–7–5) but the English translation requires no exact wordage and your own may consist of any three short lines to suit your subject.

The aimless life is the constant theme of Zen art of every kind, expressing the artist's own inner state of going nowhere in a timeless moment. All men have these moments occasionally, and it is just then that they catch those vivid glimpses of the world which cast such a glow over the intervening wastes of memory – the smell of burning leaves on a morning of autumn haze, a flight of sunlit pigeons against a thundercloud, the sound of an unseen waterfall at dusk, or the single cry of some unidentified bird in the depths of a forest . . .

From *The Way of Zen* by Alan Watts

Here are some examples:

The thief
left it behind –
the moon at the window.
Ryokan

A brushwood gate,
and for a lock –
this snail.
Basho

Dozing on horseback,
smoke from tea-fires
drifts to the moon.
Basho

In the dense mist,
what is being shouted
between hill and boat?
Issa

A fallen flower
returning to the branch?
It was a butterfly.
> Moritake

And here are some modern Haiku:

Like an ice-cream wrapper –
The last of summer
Dances down the road.
> Ian J. Burton

This empty page
Glares at me –
White with rage.
> Ian J. Burton

The delight I feel
goes stamping up the road
in the little boy's coat.
> Colin Oliver

'The poet's mind,' said T. S. Eliot, 'is in fact a receptacle for seizing and storing up numberless feelings, phrases, images, which remain there until all the particles which can unite to form a new compound are present together' (*Tradition and the Individual Talent*).

Free verse

Many writers prefer a free-style approach to poetry. The following contemporary examples show an easy conversational style which has great appeal for modern readers. Let's begin with Wendy Cope:

Tich Miller wore glasses
with elastoplast-pink frames
and had one foot three sizes larger than the other.

When they picked teams for outdoor games
she and I were always the last two
left standing by the wire-mesh fence.

We avoided one another's eyes,
stooping, perhaps, to re-tie a shoelace,
or affecting interest in the flight

of some fortunate bird, and pretended
not to hear the urgent conference:
'Have Tubby!' 'No, no, have Tich!'

Usually they chose me, the lesser dud,
and she lolloped, unselected,
to the back of the other team.

At eleven we went to different schools.
In time I learned to get my own back,
sneering at hockey-players who couldn't spell.

Tich died when she was twelve.

Tich Miller by Wendy Cope

I hear that since you left me
Things go from bad to worse,
That the Good Lord, quite rightly,
Has set a signal curse

On you, your house and lover.
(I learn, moreover, he
Proves twice as screwed-up, selfish
And sodden, dear, as me.)

They say your days are tasteless,
Flattened, disjointed, thinned,
Across the waste of my absence,
Love's skeleton, has grinned.

Perfect. I trust my sources
Of information are sound?
Or is it just some worthless rumour
I've been spreading around?

My Version by Kit Wright

And here is one of mine, first published in *The Lady*:

Look closely now, I beg you,
Hold your breath
And feast on every fragment of your world.
No flower is ever quite the same again,
The light on every stone and leaf unique.
I lost this morning, thinking back,
Feeling again the pain of yesterday;
I lost this sun, this shining grass, that bird,
Never in all my life to be reclaimed.
So feast on every morsel of your day
And hold your breath, rejoice
That you can see and feel and understand.
Look closely now, before it is too late.

Look Closely Now by Dianne Doubtfire

Sad themes, yes. But writers often express their sorrow in verse;
sometimes it can help to ease the pain.

Seeking publication

If you want to see your work in print why not explore the poetry magazines until you find a selection which are right for you. Whenever you send work out take care to choose appropriate markets for your particular themes. You will stand a much better chance of getting a book of poems accepted by a publisher if you have achieved some success in magazines.

The market for poetry is a very slender one although it has improved considerably in recent years. If your work has special quality and you are not too easily discouraged, you may reach your goal. *The Small Presses and Little Magazines of the UK and Ireland*, published by the Oriel Bookshop, The Friary, Cardiff, Wales gives a full address list of small presses publishing poetry and you will also find *The Small Press Guide* (Writers' Bookshop) very helpful.

Presentation of poetry

Send out no more than three or four poems at a time, typed centrally on sheets of A4 paper using single spacing, with double spacing between stanzas. A title sheet is not required; just put your name and address at the top right-hand corner of the first sheet, with the title and the poem underneath. There is no need to state the number of words.

I'd like to end this chapter with a poem by a boy of eight, one of the winners in a competition run by *The Guardian* for children's verses about kite-flying.

> The kite like bird floats
> Gently tugging on its string
> Hands firmly keep it.
>
> Playing with the wind,
> Having a gentle tumble,
> And winks at the sun.
>
> Could we climb the string,
> And sail around in the sky,
> For always, perhaps.
>
> A dark shadow falls
> As it crosses the bright sun,
> Strange figure passes.

It swoops low and high
With its tail dancing behind,
Then suddenly falls.

Kite quiet in the grass,
Is it dead or just sleeping?
Let us run and see.
Fly Kite by Sam Butterfield

His feelings, phrases and images were there all right. How about
yours?

Exercise 25

Write either a sonnet or three Haiku or a short poem in free verse.

Exercise 26

Write a rhyming poem in the first person where the 'I' character in
the narrative is someone completely different from yourself.

Exercise 27

Take one of the themes listed at the end of Chapter 6, Creative
Writing Competitions and write a poem of no more than 16 lines
exploring the topic. Use either rhyming or free verse.

the novel

In this chapter you will learn:
- the exciting challenge the novel offers you
- how to construct and develop your novel
- how to write a synopsis and when to approach a publisher.

The challenge

Writing a novel is one of the greatest challenges in the whole field of creative writing. It is exciting, demanding, exhausting – and deeply satisfying. There may be times when you feel you can't go on, but an inner voice will urge you to continue and if you pay attention to that voice you will somehow find the way forward. Every writer experiences frustration and hopelessness at times; the measure of your quality as a novelist is not only your imagination and your skill with words, but also your ability to persevere in the face of discouragement, to work until the pages gradually build up into a weighty pile and your book is finished.

For the purpose of this chapter we will discuss the so-called 'straight' novel, one which does not fall easily into any other category. There are, of course, many different kinds of novels – romances, science fiction, crime, teenage and so on – but I hope these guidelines will help you with whatever type you wish to write. If you decide to start an historical romance, for instance, I would advise you to read a selection of the best available and study the length, construction and style. A straight novel may be anything from 70,000 to 200,000 words and 30 chapters of roughly 2500 would give you a good average length of 75,000. Other categories vary, and you must be sure to write to an appropriate length if you want to see your work in print.

Publishers, for the most part, specialize in certain types of books and have 'slots' to fill. One of the most common reasons for refusal is that a novel 'falls between two stools'. It might be basically a romantic novel, for instance, but if it includes explicit erotic scenes which might offend the average reader of romantic fiction it would be virtually unpublishable; likewise a detective story with a love interest so strong that the book is neither a who-dun-it nor a romance. Most of us deplore these restrictions but they are an established part of the publishing world and you would be wise to heed them unless you are a writer of such brilliance that you can create your own category and take the world by storm, as Richard Adams did with *Watership Down* – after many rejections!

Before you begin a novel you might ask yourself the questions in the following sections. Finding the answers will help you to plan your book.

The theme

What is the story to be about?

In other words, what is the theme? The plot can develop later, but the theme is a matter for consideration at the outset. It can often be summed up in a single word or a short phrase: for example, betrayal, revenge, the need for independence. A book without a theme can become a mere sequence of events with no foundation, no real reason for its existence. The theme you choose should be one that concerns you deeply. It will certainly be close to your own experience but beware of writing an autobiography. You should change the characters and situations, using your imagination to create a fictitious drama. If you put yourself into a novel you will be tempted to include too many real events, losing the essential qualities of art and invention. Fiction has the appearance of reality but it must have relevance and suspense, combined into a shapely whole.

The more deeply you are affected by your theme, even to the point of obsession, the more likely you are to produce a successful book. Many of us write novels to explore the problems that trouble us, so don't be afraid to tackle a disturbing theme. Your story may be sparked off by an image – a picture of two people in confrontation, a situation of great delicacy or danger, or simply an arresting face. From this starting point you are swept into a story which builds up more and more strongly in your imagination. In cases like this, your theme may only become apparent as you progress, but you will need to keep it constantly in mind. If you lose sight of the theme you may lose that sense of unity and power which is so vital to the structure of the book.

The central character

Whose story is it?

The choice of a central character is perhaps the most important aspect of your book. This is the person your reader must care about – and care very deeply – if he is to feel involved in the story. When we read fiction we like to identify with the main character, even though he or she may be quite different from ourselves. There is also of course the fascination of the anti-hero but this is very difficult to pull off in a first novel.

As with the short story, many amateur novels are spoiled because the author chose the wrong central character. Let's say your theme is the need for independence. A woman is filled with resentment against her selfish and domineering father because he tries to prevent her from marrying the man she loves. This must surely be the woman's story. The reader will be led to identify with her, suffer with her, care about her happiness. The father's attitude will no doubt be explained and we shall understand what drives him to behave as he does, but it would be a grave mistake, in my opinion, for the author to choose him as the central character because he would not claim the reader's sympathy.

Having decided whose story it is, you should pause to consider the next important question.

What is this person's problem?

'Why does everyone have to have a problem?' you may ask. The answer is that there must be conflict or there can be no drama, no suspense, no readability. When you read the opening pages of a good novel, of whatever kind, you are drawn into the story, engrossed, eager to know the outcome. This is almost certainly because the author has presented a person with a problem. The problem faced by the hero or heroine provides the story line for the novel. It is closely bound up with the question: What is the story to be about? As the book progresses, you will drive your hero to the limits of his endurance and show the gradual development of his character. The more deeply you ponder on the problems of your characters the more you will understand about human nature. Sometimes you may find that you 'write better than you know' and look back on certain scenes with surprise and delight, marvelling at your own perception. This is a happy by-product of novel-writing: in analysing the problems of our characters we may quite unexpectedly come upon solutions to our own.

Setting

Where does it happen?

Choose localities which are close to your own experience. You will need to introduce a variety of backgrounds – the reader soon tires of the same venue – and your theme will indicate those that are appropriate to the story. Unusual settings are naturally intriguing and you should dream up a happy blend of the familiar and the exceptional (see Chapter 10, Setting).

When does it happen?

Before you begin your novel you will need to consider the time range of your book. Is the action to take place in one dramatic weekend or to cover two generations? A family saga, for instance, must be very carefully planned if you are to avoid a sprawling construction, even though you may find, as you write, that the time-span has to be increased or reduced. A story which occupies only a month is less of a problem, but in all cases I suggest that you bear in mind exactly when each scene is taking place.

It is not always easy to remember what day it is in your novel and I find it helpful to make a pencil note at the beginning of each chapter or section, for example, 'First Saturday', 'Second Thursday', 'Christmas Eve'. Changes in the weather will help you to establish a compact time-structure; heatwaves, wintry spells, gales and thunderstorms serve not only to bring atmosphere and drama into your story but also to chronicle the passing days. A confused reader is a disgruntled reader so do take care to let him know at all times Who it is, Where it is and When it is.

If you are writing an historical novel you will already be well informed about the period you have chosen, but some research is sure to be necessary; you will need to spend a good deal of time in reference libraries and museums as well as poring over library books at home and surfing the internet. Accuracy is vital. The reader's 'willing suspension of disbelief', on which all novelists rely, will be destroyed if you allow even one anachronism to slip into your story.

Construction

Where are you going to start?

I think it is true to say that this is one of the most difficult decisions any novelist has to make: at what point in the life of your main character are you to begin your story? If something of great importance occurred in his childhood, will you start with that scene in direct narrative or describe it later in flashback? Sometimes you can only solve the problem by trial and error. Flashback can be effective but it should be used sparingly; immediate action is usually much more telling than retrospect. 'John took a deep breath and threw himself into the fast-moving torrent twenty feet below' is more dramatic than 'John told me how he had taken a deep breath and thrown himself into the fast-moving torrent twenty feet below' or 'John remembered how he had ... etc.' Always 'make a scene of it' (a favourite maxim of mine) unless there are good reasons for doing otherwise. If you insert a section of flashback be sure to make the transition perfectly clear. Bear in mind that although you know exactly what is happening, and when, because you invented it, the reader knows only what he is told. I think it is a mistake to introduce flashback during the first 3000 words or so; establish a firm base in the narrative before you take the reader back.

Your first chapter should contain a big scene – or the build-up to a big scene in Chapter 2. It will probably be a confrontation between the main character and a person or situation. This conflict will embody the theme – the problem which is at the heart of your story. As a general rule, you should introduce your hero or heroine on page 1; in this way you will devise a compelling opening in which the reader identifies with him or her and hopes for a happy outcome. What the outcome is, he will only discover by following your story to the very end.

Viewpoint

I have touched on this question in Chapter 4, The Short Story. Your decision will have an important bearing on construction. If you choose the first person, you will find it easier to hold your novel within a tight framework, but there are obvious limitations: nothing can happen which is not known to your central character. If you employ the third person but adhere to one viewpoint throughout the book, you have this same problem, of course, but again it produces a strong construction. The most usual method is to write in the third person, choosing three or four viewpoint characters so that the events are seen from different angles. If you decide on this approach you will have to plan your scenes carefully, ringing the changes with a nice feeling for balance as well as drama. It is, in my opinion, a great mistake to introduce more than one viewpoint in each chapter or scene unless you signal the change with a break in the text.

An omniscient viewpoint?

'Why,' you may ask, 'can't I have a God's-eye view of all the characters, knowing and saying what they are thinking?' This is a question I often hear and my answer is this: if you leap in and out of the various characters' minds you will fragment the power of the scene and destroy its unity. Many published writers do this very thing and I can only wish they wouldn't. You will, of course, see your whole grouping objectively, but you would be wise to remain behind the eyes of your chosen viewpoint character within each scene unless you have a special reason for doing otherwise.

Plot

I dislike the word 'plot' – it suggests a contrived situation – but your book must have a strong backbone. One of the most common failings in amateur novels is a looseness of construction which allows the storyline to be lost in a welter of irrelevancies (see Chapter 4, The Short Story, '*Suspense*'). You must preserve the shape by sticking resolutely to the tale you have decided to tell, refusing to be tempted down pathways which, although attractive, lead away from the central theme. You need to tell a good story and you will find that it develops with surprising continuity, one scene growing out of another, if you allow your characters, with their individual predicaments, to lead you onwards, page by page. Try to write your novel every day, even if only for an hour or so. If you keep in touch with the narrative you will find the task much easier.

The ending

I seldom know how my novels are going to end until I get there. In my third book, *Kick a Tin Can*, I literally didn't know until I was writing the last page but one! Some novelists plan the story in great detail before they begin to write (Iris Murdoch, for instance). Others work as I do, letting the original concept change and develop as they go along. John Fowles does not plan. 'I begin,' he says, 'with an image, a ghost of an idea, nothing more, not knowing where it will lead.' Choose the way that suits you best; it's the quality of the finished book that counts.

As with the short story, beware of anti-climax. When you have brought your hero to the end of a particular phase in his life and resolved his problem, then it is time to stop.

Dramatizing a situation

The following extract from my book *The Craft of Novel-Writing* may be helpful:

> First of all, make sure that the situation you have in mind is credible and that it is vital to this novel. Then, having

decided at what point in the narrative the particular situation is to occur, lead up to it with care, creating the right atmosphere and mood. The situation might be completely unexpected but it will be convincing if you have prepared the way for it. The leading-up paragraphs, although less dramatic in themselves, make the moments of drama more telling and significant, not only by contrast, but because you are subtly building up the tension; the reader senses the approach of the storm in the stillness that precedes it.

Sometimes the preparation for a dramatic situation might begin a dozen chapters earlier – or even on the first page of the novel. Death is more tragic if the person who dies was deeply loved; joy is more intense after despair; betrayal more terrible after perfect trust ... Seize every chance for added drama, so long as everything is relevant and has, for you, the ring of truth. Make a conscious effort to intrigue and excite the reader so that your own involvement is transmitted to him and he is moved as you are moved.

In the book I have written on many aspects of the subject which cannot be included in a single chapter, and you may like to read it before you embark on a novel.

Submitting your first novel

As you browse through the publishers' section of the *Writers' and Artists' Yearbook* or *The Writer's Handbook* you will see that few if any are willing to consider a complete novel but require only the first two or three chapters plus a synopsis. Does this mean that you don't have to write the whole novel before approaching a publisher? I would say no. A *first* novelist is well advised to complete the whole book before submitting it. Why? Writing your first novel, more than any which may (or may not) follow, is a journey of discovery, fraught with uncertainties and problems which have to be solved along the way or in the editing process which follows. When you have reached the end – even though there is still work to be done, editing, re-writing etc – you might then consider submitting it to a publisher. Before you do so, re-write and polish your initial chapters and then give yourself a cooling off period of several days at least. Look at your beginning with a fresh eye and make final corrections before embarking on the submission process. An enquiry letter will establish whether or not the publisher or literary agent is willing to consider a new writer's work at the present time. If so, you will be able to submit your polished work together with a well-written synopsis by return.

Writing a synopsis

After you have written the book

It is comparatively easy to write a synopsis when your book is finished. A brief note on the contents of each chapter will help you to make a start but you should include only the broad outline of the story and an indication of the theme: be careful to avoid too much detail.

A synopsis is always written in the present tense and the wordage depends to a large extent, of course, on the length of the book to be summarized: a novel of 80,000 words might require 1000. Nevertheless, one can't be specific. A complicated plot could require much more, a simple story less. It is unlikely that a publisher will commission a novel from an unknown writer on the strength of a synopsis and a few chapters: it so often happens that the initial promise is not fulfilled. It isn't easy to keep up the standard of the first 5000 words for another 70,000 or so, and unless the publisher has proof that a particular author can maintain the high quality of a striking opening he or she will naturally be wary of risking a contract.

Before you have written the book

If you prefer to plan your stories then you will probably want to write a synopsis first. This will provide you with a framework within which to work in the months to come. The synopsis may well need to be re-written more than once as the novel progresses and new developments occur. This part of the writing process can help to clarify your thoughts as well as keeping you on track.

Commissions

A publisher, if he or she knows and admires your work, might be prepared to commission a book on the strength of a synopsis and two or three specimen chapters. In such a case you will have to summarize a book which is yet to be written, and in the case of fiction this can be a daunting task.

Many novelists, myself included, do not know how the story will develop until it is under way. It is only when I see my characters in action, hear them talking and find out how they react to the various problems which beset them, that I can plan the ending. Writing such a synopsis gives me sleepless nights, and I always add a footnote explaining to the publisher that my outline can give only a rough idea of how the story will eventually turn out. In most cases he or she will understand the difficulty and allow for changes to be made as the writing proceeds. However, initially, the publisher must be convinced that a viable novel is indeed being planned and that it will sell. If you can achieve this you are much more likely to get that longed-for commission. If you are successful, you will then receive a contract and an advance on royalties. Such an advance is usually paid in three equal instalments: on signature of the contract, on delivery of the manuscript (provided it meets with the publisher's approval) and on publication. But suppose it doesn't meet with the publisher's approval? Well, having got so far, you just work along with them until they are satisfied.

Sample fiction synopsis

The following example might be useful as a guide. I was asked by Macmillan for a synopsis of a teenage novel. They had already published my work and were prepared to commission the book if they liked the sound of it. Fortunately, they did, and *Sky Girl* came out as a Topliner Trident in 1978.

Sky Girl. A novel for teenagers by Dianne Doubtfire. Proposed length: 30,000 words.

Synopsis

The book is set in Yorkshire in the summer holidays. The story has a strong hang gliding background and will be vetted by the British Hang Gliding Association before submission, to ensure complete authenticity. Great stress will be laid on the danger of the sport and the need for extreme care and expertise.

Joy Phillips (16) a slim, athletic girl with short blonde hair has been forsaken by her boyfriend Keith, for a girl in London called Sandra. Joy and Keith were planning to be married in two years' time, when Keith would be 20, and Joy had saved up £150 by doing babysitting jobs. They have been sweethearts since childhood and three months after the break-up, when the story opens, Joy is still tormented by misery and loneliness. Her father is a merchant seaman and her mother, though kind, does not understand her depression. She tells her she will soon find another boyfriend but Joy believes she will always love Keith.

In the first chapter Joy goes by bus to a lonely hill on the Yorkshire moors, about ten miles from her home. She decides to climb the Tor and suddenly sees a hang glider flying above the rocky ridge at the top. The pilot, Dave Leeming (20) lands beside her and takes her up the hill to see the flying.

There she meets Ferdy (27), a hefty boy with a black beard who is an orphan and very insecure. He is selfish and reckless and takes needless risks, against Dave's warnings. It seems he must always try to prove himself better than everyone else and this leads to a crash and also to emotional conflicts, as Joy despises him.

Joy also meets Daphne (16), small, dark and pretty and in love with Dave. Daphne is afraid to learn to fly herself but she comes to the site in order to be with him.

Dave is a qualified hang gliding instructor, having worked at a school in Wales, and he dreams of starting a school of his own, training people to fly with safety and responsibility. Joy is keen to learn and spends the money she has saved for her wedding on a second-hand glider.

Dave teaches her to fly and she proves remarkably adept. She finds in flying a release from her misery over Keith (who now works at London Airport to be near Sandra), and she strives to reach the stage when she can fly from the top of the Tor. At last she achieves this – not without hazards – and sends a photograph of herself in flight to Keith, hoping it might revive his interest in her.

Ferdy causes some dangerous episodes and strong conflict builds up on account of his growing passion for Joy. Dave falls for her, too, and Daphne is heart-broken. Joy herself still longs for Keith, though she is very fond of Dave. She devotes all her passion to flying: it is as if she has transferred her frustrated love for Keith to her glider, a beautiful yellow craft she calls 'Butterfly'.

After weeks of practice she succeeds in breaking Ferdy's record time for staying in the air. Dave is delighted but Ferdy is outraged and plots revenge. His plan turns against him, with traumatic results, owing to the intervention of Dave's younger brother, Mark (12).

The final drama occurs when Joy is flying on a windy day against Dave's advice. While she is soaring she hears a familiar shout and sees Keith on the hillside below, waving to her. Joy loses concentration and is unable to deal correctly with a sudden gust of wind. She crashes badly and is taken to hospital with a broken leg and a broken arm. Keith visits her and explains that he has finished with Sandra and wants Joy back. She is rapturous until she tells him she wants to carry on flying when she has recovered. Keith makes it clear that he will not allow her to do so, and she recognizes his dictatorial nature and lack of understanding.

One day Keith and Dave visit the hospital at the same time and, seeing them together, she realizes that it is Dave she really loves.

In the last scene Joy is able to walk on crutches and she and Dave are happily planning the Hang Gliding School they will one day run together.

When I came to write the book, all kinds of unexpected dramas developed. Joy's mother was fiercely opposed to hang gliding and Joy had to keep her flying a secret. And it was not Keith who came to the Tor and shouted at her, causing her to crash: it was her mother, alerted by Ferdy. (More conflict – the very life-blood of fiction!)

There was no problem with the publisher about the changes and I was asked to write a sequel, *Sky Lovers*, which was also commissioned on the strength of a synopsis and published in 1981. This, too, was considerably altered in the writing and no author need worry too much about subsequent changes so long as the basic story remains the same.

Best selling genres

One of the things you will need to tell the publisher is which genre or category your book falls into.

The straight novel and the thriller are currently the most popular genres, between them they accounted for nearly 60 per cent of paperback sales in the year 2000 and occupied over 50 places in the Top 100 (which also included 12 non-fiction titles). (Figures source: Alex Hamilton's *Top Hundred Chart of 2000 Paperback Fastsellers*, which first appeared in *The Guardian*.) Other best selling categories include romance, saga, historical, crime, adventure, juvenile, mystery, and anthology. There are two unfamiliar categories – 'town girl' novels – tales of modern city women, for example, Helen Fielding's *Bridget Jones's Diary* and 'town boy' novels – tales of the modern man, for example, Mike Gayle's *Mr Commitment*.

If you are wondering where the science fiction and the western genres are, well, they didn't make the charts in the year 2000 which doesn't mean they are extinct but is merely an indication of the picture that year.

Choosing a publisher

1 Using the *Writers' and Artists' Yearbook* or *The Writer's Handbook*, search for publishers who handle not just fiction but fiction in your particular category.
2 Decide on a short list.
3 If a web address is available visit the site and explore it fully for any information which will be helpful.
4 If submission guidelines are available request a copy (send stamped-addressed envelope) or download them from the internet.
5 Request (separately) current/forthcoming retail catalogues for their fiction list.
6 Research and evaluate the information you have gathered and draw up your short list of publishers.
7 Consider a query letter as your initial approach if this seems appropriate.
8 As with the non-fiction book submission outlined in Chapter 19, prepare your submission package with a great deal of time and care. Do not rush this process. Be patient.

Exercise 28

If you have in mind a novel you would like to write, answer the preceding six questions in note form. For reference, here are the six questions again:

1 What is the story to be about?
2 Whose story is it?
3 What is this person's problem?
4 Where does it happen?
5 When does it happen?
6 Where are you going to start?

Exercise 29

From your notes above, write a detailed chapter-by-chapter synopsis for your own use to guide you through the novel.

16

writing for children

Creative writing presents us with a paradox and it's one which becomes even more apparent when considering writing for children. On the one hand, of course, we want to give imagination and creativity free range but on the other hand we're advised to write within a framework of guidelines and publisher's requirements. When writing for children, should you, then, research the market first, get to know all the categories, the reading and age ranges, latest trends, etc., and then switch on your imagination commanding it to produce a publishable piece of fiction intended, say, for a nine-year-old; or do you just write blindly without reference to the market only to find that there isn't a market for a teen novel of 187,000 words or a 53-page picture book? Of course, neither approach is satisfactory.

If your passion is to write for a young audience then you must follow it, passionately, imaginatively, freely. But by gaining a general knowledge of the market as you go along you will be able to direct your work, adapting and refining it accordingly before you are finally ready to approach a publisher. You will then stand a much better chance of having your manuscript considered by a publisher.

The readership and the writer

In *general* you need to have some idea of the age of your readers before you begin, remembering that, on a higher level, the best children's writers simply *write,* addressing themselves to another human being, of whatever age, who will respond with pleasure. 'Whatever you have in hand, write it as simply as you can, and the material itself will dictate the nature of the audience,' says the much-loved author Jill Paton Walsh.

When Philip Pullman, author of *The Amber Spyglass*, was asked in *Young Writer* magazine, 'Did you decide to write for children or did it just work out that way?', he replied, 'I don't think I write for anyone, actually. I just tell the story the way it wants to be told. If children read it, fine. If adults read it, fine. If horses want to read it, that's OK, too.' Later in the interview he went on to say, 'The problem with saying that any book is for this or that group is that when you say that, you also seem to be saying that it's not for any other. And I want my audience to be as large and inclusive as possible.'

The Amber Spyglass won the prestigious Whitbread Book Award 2001 and is the first children's book to do so. It is the third book in Philip Pullman's trilogy *His Dark Materials*. If you would like to visit the *Young Writer* website the address is www.mystworld.com/youngwriter

You and your audience

I think you must feel at ease with children – indeed, have a childlike quality in your own nature – in order to write for them successfully. You should also be closely in touch with today's youngsters, however clearly you recall your own childhood. Things are very different now. Their language changes constantly – a new television cartoon series can result in mystifying additions to a child's vocabulary, quite apart from the regular influx of jargon new technology brings.

Telling stories

Let's assume you have an idea you are burning to explore and develop and you know roughly the age group you would like to reach. Here are the main writing skills you will need to employ along the way. Later in the chapter we will take a look at the marketing side of the equation.

Pace

It is very important to keep the action going and make sure that there is excitement on every page. This applies to the domestic story which is closely related to the reader's experience as well as to thrillers, science-fiction, fantasy and adventure. Movement and colour are key words for children's fiction and you must present your story in a way which will grip the attention on the very first page and hold it till the last. Short sentences, short paragraphs and short chapters will help to achieve this result. The time and place must be unmistakable and the characters clearly defined.

Characterization

Beginners often make the mistake of writing about a child who lacks individuality – kind, intelligent, good-looking, but in no way *unique*. Think about your young characters as deeply as you would for an adult story and create a hero or heroine who comes to life as a full-blooded person with strong individuality. Readers like to identify with the main character so choose a child who is a little older than your intended readership. And if your story requires a villain then he, she or it must be utterly villainous and scarily believable within the context of the story. Take a look at the 'baddies' in Roald Dahl's stories and the way he describes them and you will see what I mean. Here's an example from *The BFG* (Big Friendly Giant):

> The Bloodbottler was a gruesome sight. His skin was a reddish-brown. There was black hair sprouting on his chest and arms and on his stomach. The hair on his head was long and dark and tangled. His foul face was round and squashy-looking. The eyes were tiny black holes. The nose was small and flat. But the mouth was huge. It spread across the face almost ear to ear, and it had lips that were like two gigantic purple frankfurters lying one on top of the other. Craggy yellow teeth stuck out between the two purple frankfurter lips, and rivers of spit ran down over the chin.

> It was not in the least difficult to believe that this ghastly brute ate men, women and children every night.

From The BFG by Roald Dahl

Bear in mind that youngsters like their 'goodies' and 'baddies' quite distinct so that they know for certain whose side to be on!

The main character need not be human. Animals are perennial favourites. Any creature from a tortoise to a pterodactyl will be taken to a child's heart if you tell a good story about it and appreciate the need for distinct animal characterization. Notice how Richard Adams achieves this:

> The first rabbit stopped in a sunny patch and scratched his ear with rapid movements of his hind-leg... He looked as though he knew how to take care of himself. There was a shrewd, buoyant air about him as he sat up, looked around and rubbed both front paws over his nose. As soon as he was satisfied that all was well, he laid back his ears and set to work on the grass.

> His companion seemed less at ease. He was small, with wide, staring eyes and a way of raising and turning his head which suggested not so much caution as a kind of ceaseless, nervous tension. His nose moved continually and when a bumble-bee flew humming to a thistle bloom behind him, he jumped and spun round with a start that sent two nearby rabbits scurrying for holes before the nearest, a buck with black-tipped ears, recognized him and returned to feeding.

'Oh, it's only Fiver,' said the black-tipped rabbit, 'jumping at blue-bottles again ...'

From *Watership Down* by Richard Adams

The following scene is from Tessa Krailing's *A Dinosaur Called Minerva*.

'Don't do that. Please don't do that!' Sprog raised the stone above his head.

'I don't mean you any harm. Please don't throw that stone.'

He stared unbelievingly at the creature. 'Are you a dragon?' he asked fearfully.

'What's a dragon?' The mournful eyes gazed at him.

'Well, it's a ...' Sprog searched for the right words. 'I don't know really, but you do look very much like one. At least – er, how much more of you is there underneath the water?'

The creature glanced down. 'Quite a lot.'

'Can you breathe fire?'

'I'm not sure. I've never tried. Quite honestly, I don't really feel like trying, not just now. I haven't been at all well lately.'

'I'm sorry to hear that,' said Sprog politely. 'I hope it's nothing serious?'

'The most frightful toothache. I've hardly been able to get any sleep at all. Can you see anything?' It opened its mouth wide, revealing a hideous array of teeth. Sprog pressed back against the cave wall again. 'It's somewhere around the left-hand side at the bottom, towards the back.'

Dialogue

Notice how the dialogue between Sprog and Minerva in the scene above establishes the friendship between them after a tense and alarming beginning.

Always introduce plenty of dialogue, but beware of slang that will date. Avoid four-letter words; children don't mind them in the least but parents and teachers do. Introduce your characters one at a time and don't have too many.

When Jill Paton Walsh was asked by a young reader, 'Do you put real people in your books?', she gave this interesting reply:

I hope the people in my books are real to you. They are real to me. Sometimes I seem to be able to hear them talking in my head. I don't make up what they say; I just listen and write it down. But they aren't portraits of people that I know in real life. You can't put actual people into books, because you don't know enough about them.

The reality factor

Right must always triumph in the end and the young hero (or heroine) should find a way out of his difficulties *by his own efforts;* never let an adult be the one to sort things out. The days are past, thank goodness, when parents, teachers and the police had to be portrayed as beyond reproach. Children watch television news, catch the headlines on the internet and when they read stories about the real world, they want truth not hypocrisy. They are upset by too much suffering and distress for the main character if he is a child like themselves but they enjoy horror if it is not too close to their own experience. A child will be far more distraught while reading about a little boy who loses his mother on a railway station than about a pirate who is boiled in oil!

Humour

Humour is important but remember that young children do not understand sarcasm. They all love slap-stick and revel (like the rest of us) in the downfall of unpleasant people in authority. Roald Dahl's books are scary in places but they are funny too. The humour in J. K. Rowling's *Harry Potter* series plays just as important a role as the thrills and the excitement.

Endings

On the whole, children prefer happy endings; whenever I give a talk at a school I ask for a show of hands on this question. I also ask about first or third person narrative and it seems they have no preference provided it's a good story and they can easily relate to the main character.

Descriptive writing

Description of characters and places must be kept to a minimum and introduced in small doses, interspersed with plenty of action and dialogue. In order to make your images vivid and colourful you may find it helpful to picture your scenes in terms of illustrations for the book; you need a strong visual approach when you are writing for young people. Above all, write with clarity and simplicity. And that, of course, is good advice for creative writing in general.

Vocabulary and context

In writing for children, the words you use should, in general, fall within their normal vocabulary, but the occasional long word will give the story an added zest provided that the word is not vital to the meaning. If writing for the under-sevens for example the sentence, 'Susan saw an adolescent boy climb into the boat' would be wrong, but 'Susan saw the boat rock perilously as the little boy jumped into it' is quite acceptable. A child who doesn't understand the word 'adolescent' cannot picture the scene correctly, whereas the meaning of perilously is implicit in the phrase and can be skipped, although the reader (or listener) will probably remember the word and expand his vocabulary.

Non-fiction books

Once upon a time a non-fiction book was a flat assembly of pages filled with text and a collection of pictures and drawings to illustrate the subject. Things have changed.

These days you are likely to encounter an array of flaps, pop-ups, holes, wheels and inflatables springing from the pages, plus exhibition standard photographs and stunningly vivid illustrations which amuse, instruct and surprise. All this is co-ordinated to give a sense of exploration and fun designed to entertain youngsters and adults *together* in the quest for knowledge on a focussed topic.

There is an endless variety of subjects to choose from: Planet Earth, sports, hobbies, pets, computers, making things, and learning new facts about almost anything – from the way a spider weaves its web to the rings of Saturn. Whatever you decide upon, it must be written in a direct, lively style, friendly and conversational, with all your information logically and clearly presented. If you can write on a topic which has not yet been covered for children, you are in a splendid position to produce a successful book. After thorough research, planning and detailed market research it is advisable to approach your chosen publisher with a synopsis and sample chapter before you begin.

Collaboration

My very first book was written in collaboration with a friend. We discovered, by chance, that there was no book on stamp-collecting for very young children. Kay Horowicz and I wanted to remedy this and we decided to write a book for five- to seven-year-olds entitled *Fun with Stamps*. She was an expert philatelist with a valuable collection, but not a writer; I only collected stamps in a half-hearted fashion but I had become successful in selling articles. Neither of us could have written the book alone but together we thought we could do it. It was published by Hutchinson in 1957 and stayed in print for 20 years!

We worked on a fifty-fifty basis all along, sharing the work, the expenses and – later – the royalties. She supplied the information in note form, and I wrote it up. I had never written for that age-group but I studied the market and it worked. Kay died many years ago but she will always live in those pages and I shall never forget the happy hours we spent with our heads together, comparing notes until we were both quite satisfied that we had done the best we could.

Perhaps, as I did, you can find someone with specialized knowledge who is willing to join forces so that you can produce a book together. (See Chapter 19, The Non-Fiction Book for more information on collaboration.)

Articles and short stories

Apart from books, there is a place for short articles of 1000 words or so in annuals, in some comics and on the children's pages of various periodicals. Consult *The Writers' and Artists' Yearbook* or *The Writer's Handbook* for current requirements and study the market before planning your article. You must, of course, know the required length and style in order to please an editor, and a trip to the newsagent could repay you well. Study the markets carefully and tailor your work accordingly.

Getting to know the children's book market

Internet bookshops such as Amazon (www.amazon.co.uk) and BOL, which stands for Books On Line (www.bol.com) have access to around 1,500,000 titles. You can browse through the categories, search by title, by author, read a blurb of the book and reader reviews, see the bestseller charts, even discover how many printed pages the book has and all without leaving home. Research has never been so easy! But there is nothing like a real bookshop or a library and having a book actually in your hands – especially important when studying children's books.

Study the length, format and subject matter of the books which are popular, those which are most frequently bought and borrowed. Talk to teachers and librarians, but most of all *talk to children*. Ask them what they enjoy the most and why. Read their favourite authors and find out what it is that makes the books appealing. One thing is certain, you will discover that successful writers never 'talk down'; the slightest hint of a patronizing or moralizing approach will ruin your chances of success.

Age categories

Remember, these are meant to help not hinder. They provide useful guidelines for publishers, booksellers, parents, teachers and writers. Here is a rough breakdown, although bear in mind that the age ranges vary slightly between different publishers and booksellers.

0–5 years

A very hard section for the new writer to break into. Picture books and board books. Hardback books are ideal for small children, not only because they are durable but because the child will learn from an early age to handle books with care and keep them (relatively) free from chocolate and peanut butter. Bright, vibrant illustrations with a variety of approaches including touch and feel books presenting a variety of textures to experience and holes and compartments built into the book for little fingers to explore.

Children at the older end of this category are ready for stories and to learn about animals and the world around them.

Illustrations

As a writer you need only concern yourself with the words, but you should consider the plan of the page spreads; your wording must give rise to suitable illustrations at regular intervals. The publisher will organize the pictures if he accepts your manuscript, although your suggestions will receive careful consideration. Royalties are shared between author and artist.

5–7 years

In this section of the bookshop you will find 'read alone' as well as 'read aloud' books designed for this age grouping. The child is more independent by now and may be choosing what to read whilst retaining old favourites. Books containing separate stories about the same characters, either human or animal, are especially popular with the very young and lend themselves to bedtime reading. A dozen stories of 800 words each – about five minutes' reading time – would be a suitable length.

7–9 years

Longer texts, of 1500–8000 words, possibly broken down into chapters for the longer lengths, are suitable for this age group. The stories are usually supported by black and white illustrations which help to enhance the story as well as breaking up the text.

You will find individual titles under an overall series title. A publisher's catalogue will help you to verify the various lengths and reading abilities offered by the series. Writers' guidelines may also be available from individual publishers.

9–12 years

By now the child will be choosing what to read next and may be branching out into specific genres such as science-fiction, fantasy, horror, history and non-fiction. Lengths may go up to 40,000 words depending on the type of book and the publisher.

It might be helpful to see how Waterstone's categorizes some well known classic books in its *Guide to Children's Books*:

Winnie-the-Pooh by A. A. Milne age 5+
Fantastic Mr Fox by Roald Dahl age 6+
The Hodgeheg by Dick King-Smith age 7+
The Worst Witch by Jill Murphy age 7+
Harry Potter and the Philosopher's Stone by J. K. Rowling 8+
Anne of Green Gables by L. M. Montgomery 9+
The Silver Sword by Ian Serrallier 9+
Stig of the Dump by Clive King age 9+
Goodnight Mister Tom by Michelle Magorian age 10+

The Hobbit by J. R. R. Tolkien age 10+
The Diary of a Young Girl by Anne Frank age 12+
I Capture the Castle by Dodie Smith age Teen
Refugee Boy by Benjamin Zephaniah age Teen

No one is suggesting that an eager child would have to wait until they were ten before reading *The Hobbit* or that if you hadn't read *Winnie-the-Pooh* by the time you were six you'd missed the boat! Now let's move on to the final category: the teen or young adults group.

Young adults

This is a big category and can span the age range between very bright 11-year-olds at one end and 16-year-olds at the other. It is one of the most exciting and challenging areas of writing but before we explore it further here is a note of caution. Let me quote from Transworld's *Guidelines for Children's Books*. 'The Young Adult book market is one of the hardest in which to sell successfully. Over the years we have published some exciting and original books for these readers, and achieved some very successful results, but again we do have to be extremely selective in this area.'

I began this chapter by saying that if you could bring passion and imagination to a subject then you will have a chance no matter how difficult the prospects seem to begin with. If this is your chosen area you will probably already know, instinctively perhaps, who your target audience is. Here is a rough guide to help you further.

Age groups

The readership is sometimes subdivided into 'teenagers' (11–13) and 'young adults' (13–15+). If you consider the difference between an 11-year-old and a 16-year-old it does make sense.

Topics

Under the banner of Young Adult Fiction there are many sub-categories to explore. Take, for example, the way amazon.co.uk arranges its Young Adult titles: Adventure and Thrillers; Horror; Love and Romance; Mysteries; School and Sports Fiction; Science-Fiction and Fantasy; Social Issues – Fiction. Social Issues

– Fiction is further broken down into Drug Use and Abuse; Family; Homosexuality; Prejudice and Violence.

Fantasy, witchcraft and vampire books are very popular, especially those with a TV tie-in such as *Buffy the Vampire Slayer.*

Length

The length of a Young Adult novel can be between 25,000 and 60,000 words depending on the age of the audience and the type of book.

Style

Strong characterization is vital together with a page turning ability to involve the reader who must be able to identify with the main character. The flow of the narrative and dialogue should instil a compulsive need to know what happens to the hero or heroine.

Keeping in touch

To write for young adults you need to be able to empathize with them and understand their problems and attitudes. It's also true to say that writers observe more than they imagine. If you have no young adults in your family try to form friendships with as many as possible, talking about the issues which concern them.

Read Young Adult novels especially in the area you are interested in. Watch television programmes for and about young people. Listen to pop radio, paying special attention to the patter of the disc jockeys. Listen also to the issues raised by young people in radio phone-in programmes.

If you write an absorbing tale with warmth and understanding you will give your readers something of value to think about, long after the excitement of the story is forgotten.

As you can see from the category list, almost any subject is permissible, with the eternal proviso that it is treated with delicacy and compassion. Youngsters who are going through a disturbed period in their lives, often with no one to confide in, can be comforted and helped by stories which deal sympathetically with problems similar to their own.

Kate Cann, author of the trilogy comprising *Diving In*, *In the Deep End* and *Sink or Swim*, has this to say on the Women's Press Website: (www.the-womens-press.com):

I wrote *Diving In* because I was fed up with teenage books treating sex and relationships in only two ways: deeply serious stuff about unwanted pregnancy, rape or abuse; and fake romantic fluffy stuff with impossible characters. I wanted to write something realistic about the power of falling in love and sex – and I wanted the final message to be a positive one. Coll is a strong, funny, independent heroine who has to deal with being poleaxed by Art, the object of her passion. She's crazy about him but she's not about to abandon everything she is just to win his approval and keep him. People either love Art or hate him. I've got a very soft spot for him and I think it's entirely believable that Coll falls for him as hard as she does!

Kate Cann's trilogy is published by The Women's Press in the *Livewire* series.

Exercise 30
Write a story of 800 words for a child under seven, creating a character, animal or human, which will inspire deep affection in the reader

Exercise 31
Develop further the character created in Exercise 28 (Chapter 15, The Novel) having in mind a novel for young adults.

writing for radio

In this chapter you will learn:
- how to get started with the radio talk and short story
- how to use the medium of radio for drama
- the layout and presentation of a radio script.

Radio, unlike computers and television, doesn't require our fixed attention. Radio is for the ears and the imagination alone, that's the difference. Its portability means that radio can be enjoyed anywhere. We can listen and be involved whilst doing something else, for example, driving, working in the garden, relaxing in the bath or painting the ceiling. During the running time of a single play we might have engaged in all of those activities!

Spoken-word radio, such as the BBC's Radio 4, is an active rather than a passive medium; we become involved when a programme catches and holds our attention. Two people can listen to the same radio drama and have completely different 'pictures' of the cast of characters and setting. This level of intimacy offers an exciting and creative challenge whether you are writing fiction or non-fiction for the medium. Let's start with the radio talk.

What is a radio talk?

It is a piece of writing, similar to a magazine article or feature but specially written for radio. It could be a short contribution of, say, five minutes for inclusion in a magazine programme – for example, BBC Radio 4's *Woman's Hour, You and Yours* or *Home Truths*. Other examples of radio-magazine programmes can be found on independent national radio, local radio as well as digital and internet radio channels such as *Oneword*. You will have your own favourites. Studying them, from a writer's point of view, will identify the nature of the programmes together with the style, length and general subject matter of the items included.

A radio talk could also be a single-topic programme in its own right, 15 minutes in length or more. Talks are most often based on personal experiences but must be of general interest to a wider audience and must be specially written for the medium.

An arresting opening is, as ever, vitally important but perhaps even more so on radio; the listener will soon switch off if he is not immediately attracted by what you have to say and the way you say it. Short sentences will work better on radio than complicated ones with sub-clauses.

Your writing style should be chatty and conversational. A colloquial turn of phrase will also help, for example, abbreviating 'would not' into 'wouldn't', 'cannot' into 'can't', will help to avoid stilted, formal phrasing.

Bear in mind that the listener is unable to glance back over the text as the magazine reader can and, therefore, your writing must be very clear and explicit. Don't say: 'Standing by the window, fingering his tie, and looking like a nervous schoolboy, stood my old headmaster.' For radio, write it straight: 'My old headmaster stood by the window, fingering his tie, and looking like a nervous schoolboy.' It is wise to avoid starting a sentence with the present participle, certainly for radio, and indeed on most occasions.

Read your work aloud before you type it finally; in this way you can check that it is conversational rather than literary and also that the timing is correct. At a speech rate of about 135/140 words a minute a sheet of A4 typescript would take approximately two minutes to read aloud. The BBC runs efficiently on time because everyone is geared to think in seconds rather than minutes. Your scripts *must* be accurately timed; read quite slowly with adequate pauses between sentences. Most people are inclined to hurry. Err on the long side rather than the reverse; almost every piece of writing is improved by cutting, but padding can be disastrous.

A cassette recorder is, of course, immensely useful in radio writing (and research). Some people find they can speak their talks straight on to tape, transcribing and editing them later. This, they feel, ensures a chatty style. For me it would ensure interminable silence, but we all have our special gifts and weaknesses, and must find our different ways accordingly. You could submit your talk on tape as well as on paper though it is unlikely that its recording quality would be of broadcast standard.

If you can write in a humorous vein you're half way there, and talks that are helpful to listeners are also in demand (for example, the overcoming of health or emotional problems). These must be written without a trace of self-pity or sentimentality, and this, of course, applies to all good writing. Listen to the programmes as often as you can and analyse them to find out what you might contribute.

Talks are always read over the air by their authors and you would have to undergo a voice test at the microphone before your manuscript can be finally accepted. This is nothing to worry about and most people pass without difficulty.

Exercise 32

Drawing on personal experience, choose a topic which you think would be of interest to a general audience. Aim for a running time of exactly five minutes.

The radio short story

The Afternoon Reading is a short story slot on BBC Radio 4 every weekday afternoon from 15.30–15.45. There are fewer opportunities here now for new writers than there used to be as most of the stories broadcast are by established writers. However, for that very reason, it is recommended as a valuable part of your researches into the radio medium and your continuing exploration of fiction writing techniques. You will hear excellent short stories written by leading writers, for example, Michèle Roberts and Helen Dunmore. The stories are superbly read by some of our best actors.

How to analyse a radio story

Select a story. Record it onto tape. Listen to the story without pause. This will give you the plot and shape of the story and will hopefully enable you to enjoy it as the author intended.

Shortly after hearing the story for the first time write a précis of it beginning with the words 'This is the story of...' and limit yourself to no more than 60 words in total. Now, go back over the story and answer the following ten questions:

1 Was the story told in the first or the third person?
2 What was established in the first minute of the story?
3 How many characters were there in total and who was the main character?
4 How did the writer describe the setting of the story?
5 What was the problem or source of conflict?
6 How was dialogue used?
7 What was the time span of the story?
8 How did the beginning develop in the later stages of the story?
9 Why did the story end where it did?
10 What was the theme?

Exercise 33

Analyse a 15-minute radio story, identifying the structure of the story and the writing techniques used.

Listen to a wide range of stories and repeat the above process for each. This will help you to identify and understand many of the techniques of fiction writing whether for radio or not.

Writing a story for radio: a few hints and tips

The first person singular is particularly appropriate for a radio story as it gives the impression of someone confiding a personal experience. Keep to a single viewpoint, seeing the situation only through the eyes of your central character. Other characters will speak and react, but we shall not know their thoughts; the listener must identify with your chosen protagonist from the beginning to the end. This advice holds good for any story, but for radio it is particularly important.

Limit the number of characters involved in your story to a maximum of four. The story should revolve around one person's problem and a single period of time. As with the radio talk, avoid long, convoluted sentences and don't include even a single dialogue exchange which does not advance the story or deepen the characterization – preferably *both at the same time*. Jumps of several days or weeks are usually unsatisfactory in a short story.

As with the magazine story, try to make your ending both unexpected and inevitable. A sombre theme need not mean that the story is depressing. The courage and imagination people show in the face of trouble is always an inspiration.

The length required for a 15-minute story is about 2250 words but don't work to a set number of words, you must read your story aloud to time it properly. The 15-minute radio story is in fact fourteen-and-a-half minutes to allow for the announcement of the title, your name, the name of the reader and the producer.

Beginning your radio story

The first minute is decisive. The listener will either switch off or settle down to enjoy himself, depending on those vital 150 words. Take these two openings:

> Whenever I see a green sports car I feel an overwhelming desire to smash the windscreen. It's all because of Molly Shipton, who won the village beauty contest last summer.

> 'One morning in late autumn I was standing alone on the platform of a country station in Wiltshire. I had five minutes to wait before my train came in and I occupied myself by counting the pigeons on the roof of a nearby house. It was a

cold day and as I stamped my feet to keep warm, the pigeons took flight, their sudden movement the only stir in the still, frosty air.

Most people would have tuned to another station by the end of example 2. Example 1, I think, is sufficiently promising to make the listener stay with it. Sports cars and beauty queens have high interest value. Country stations and rows of pigeons have none unless there is some other factor to indicate an intriguing development. 'Ah,' says the author, 'but there is an intriguing development when the train comes in.' 'What?' I ask, 'Five minutes later?' The solution, of course, is to start the story when the train comes in, to begin when the kettle is beginning to boil, not when it is filled at the tap.

Exercise 34

Now it's your turn. Write the first three minutes of a radio story (about 450 words). If you go on to complete the story and feel it is good enough to submit, see the section below 'Sending your work to the BBC' for details of the New Writing Initiative.

Further information

The BBC World Service also broadcasts short stories and occasionally invites non-UK based writers to contribute manuscripts as well as organizing short story competitions. Visit their website:
www.bbc.co.uk/worldservice/arts/features/howtowrite/.
The useful 'How To Write...' section also covers the radio play, the novel, memoirs and screenplay writing plus advice from successful writers.

The radio play

The possibilities are endless. At no extra cost you can set your scene in medieval Britain, on a tropical island, in an aircraft flying over the South Pole or at the top of the Eiffel Tower. All the listener has to do is to close his eyes and allow you to take him there. All *you* have to do is to fill those blank sheets of A4 paper with the right sounds, speeches and silences.

The BBC's New Writing Initiative represents an active attempt to find and encourage new writers as the following quote from the

BBC website shows. 'We are constantly on the lookout for writers of any age, with potential for BBC TV and Radio Drama to take part in these initiatives.'

Paul Abbott, writer of the BBC TV series *Clocking Off*, says:

> My first professional writing contracts were all single plays for Radio 4 which is still a fertile forum for testing your strengths. Radio produces more comedy, drama and sketch shows than all TV channels put together. (It's relatively inexpensive so you're allowed to experiment, thank God!)

The Writers' Room, www.bbc.co.uk

But to succeed, as in any other branch of creative writing, you must understand and respond to the particular challenges of the medium you are working in. The craft is specialized but not too difficult to master if you have a good story to tell and a gift for writing dialogue.

Getting started

Now let's get down to the practicalities. A radio play *must* be written specially for the medium. It's no use sending a stage play to the BBC in the hope that they will fall in love with it and adapt it themselves. You must learn the techniques and produce a typescript which proves that you know your job.

Sequences

Radio plays are divided into sequences in much the same way as television plays are divided into scenes. Each sequence must flow into the one that follows, leaving no doubt in the listener's mind as to where and when the action is taking place. Every sequence should end with a 'fade' or a 'cut'. The passage of time may be indicated by music, silence or some other device of your own invention. Sequences may vary in length from just a few seconds to several minutes, depending on the content. This is one of the ways in which you can introduce variety, along with change of pace, volume of sound, exterior and interior settings – and above all contrasts in character. Each sequence has its own natural length beyond which the listener's interest will waver.

Characterization

Beware of creating characters who are too much alike. As your play moves from one sequence to another the identity of the characters involved must be unmistakable at all times, so avoid having two young men or two young women unless you devise some obvious difference of temperament or vernacular.

Characters will not necessarily say what they think directly. They don't or won't automatically respond to what has been said to them preferring perhaps to avoid the issue or misunderstand what's being said. Characters almost certainly won't have the same clear view of themselves as you, the author, have. They may not be aware of motivations and agendas either in themselves or in other characters and consequently their dialogue will reflect this.

Dialogue

As we have seen in Chapter 9, Dialogue there's a lot more to it than just people talking. Every line of dialogue must make its contribution to the story as a whole *and* move the plot forwards – hopefully without the reader/listener even realizing it and yet whilst holding their attention!

Avoid strong dialect; regional speech may be suggested by a turn of phrase but be sure you are really familiar with the region you choose. Listen to a radio play, especially one on tape, and then listen again taking note of the various tasks the dialogue performs from filling in the back-story of the characters, that is, subtle references to what happened before the play began, to characterization e.g. a conversation between two people which characterizes a third.

Timing

There is no reliable way to estimate the length of a play by the number of pages or the number of words. You must time your play by reading it aloud and 'walking through it'. It must fit into one of the available slots, but write it a minute or two too long to allow for trimming in rehearsal. It should on no account be too short; as noted earlier, cutting is much easier than inserting new material.

Your play must be written with a keen visual sense. The listener will have a clear mental image if you write your speeches well; for

instance, *'What a lovely dress – I've always adored red velvet.'*
'Just look at that moon – I'm sure it's twice its usual size!'

You must also be aware of atmosphere – scents and feelings that
help to bring the scene to life for the listener. ('Oh, that lilac – I
can smell it from here.' 'Tom – your socks need washing!' 'What's
that hole in the floor? It looks as if a rat might come out at any
moment.')

Further research

Listen to radio plays as often as possible. Study the technique with
great attention, making notes as you listen. Time the length of the
sequences and analyse the ways in which they lead from one to
another.

Example 1

DONALD:	I'll see you tomorrow, then – half twelve on the little bridge by the church.
JOAN:	Yes – I'll bring a picnic.
DONALD:	Suppose it rains?
JOAN:	Misery! It won't rain.
	(FADE TO SOUND OF HEAVY RAIN)
DONALD:	What did I tell you!

The scene is unmistakably changed to the next day on the bridge.

Example 2

MUM:	Where's our Meg? It's after ten.
DAD:	(Angrily) If she's playing darts with that Joe Scott again, I'll half kill her.
(CUT TO SOUND OF DARTS HITTING DARTBOARD)	
MEG:	Come on, Joe – you can do better than that.

Example 3

BERYL:	We're all at the mercy of our moods. There's nothing we can do about it.
JAMES:	Nonsense, darling. There's plenty you can do if you really make an effort.
BERYL:	What do *you* know about it? I'll ask Dr Wells this afternoon.
	(FADE TO)
BERYL:	Doctor, may I ask you something? My husband says you can do something about your moods if you 'make an effort' as he puts it. But you can't, can you? It's all tied up with glands and things, isn't it?

Note that it is essential to insert 'this afternoon' in Beryl's second speech, otherwise the time would not be established clearly; it might be a week or a month later.

An understanding of the precise difference between 'fade' and 'cut' is not important at this stage so long as your story is clearly expressed; the producer will deal with such details once your play is accepted.

Plays can be of 30, 45, 60, 75 or 90 minutes' duration but 30 minutes is probably the most suitable length for your first attempt. Study the *Radio Times* for current requirements.

Sound effects

Keep your sound effects to an absolute minimum. The opening and closing of a door need only be mentioned if someone slams it in rage or it creaks open stealthily at the dead of night. Beware, too, of the sounds of drinks being poured. If it's poison, *then* let us hear it! (This is an exaggeration, but it makes the point.) Amateur writers often make their characters perform actions which cannot register on the air except in long, unexplained silences; they forget that the listener can't see what is happening. The accepted abbreviation for sound effects in a script is FX.

Directions

Avoid 'stage' directions; any important movement should be written into the dialogue, (for example, 'David – for God's sake – you're doing ninety!' rather than 'David accelerates the car to ninety miles an hour' which would be useless in a radio script. You could introduce a narrator who conveys information to the listener but it would be best to avoid this method for your first play as it is all too easy to overdo the narrator's role and find yourself with a semi dramatized short story instead of a radio play. Never use a narrator unless there is no other way of writing your play effectively.

Script layout

The script layout for a radio drama has changed in recent years, moving more in style towards the television script layout. I am showing the most recent layout as requested by the BBC's New Writing Initiative on their web page.
www.bbc.co.uk/writersroom/guidelines.

F/X	SCENE 2. INT. JIM'S LOUNGE – DAY

MARY: It's no good fuming and raging like that, Daddy. Why don't you do something practical about it? Call a public meeting or something?

JIM: A public meeting? Yes – all right – that's a good idea. I'll get some posters printed. Yes – a public meeting...

(FADE TO)

F/X	SCENE 3. INT. VILLAGE HALL – NIGHT

SOUNDS OF CHATTERING AND CHAIR-SCRAPING IN THE VILLAGE HALL BEFORE THE MEETING STARTS. OCCASIONAL SNATCHES ARE HEARD: 'Quite a turn out'; 'Hope they keep it short'; 'About time something was done'. THERE IS A SHARP KNOCKING ON A TABLE AND THE BABBLE DIES DOWN.

JIM : Good evening, everybody. And welcome. I'm sure we can all agree about these heavy lorries. It's not like politics and that kind of thing – it's entirely for the good of the community –

(LAUGHTER)

I'll ask my daughter to explain our plan for some positive action to keep these damned juggernaughts away from our village. Mary?

(APPLAUSE)

MARY : (BRIGHTLY) Hello everyone. Before I begin I'd like to take the opportunity of paying tribute to the good work done by –

MAN: Cut the cackle, sweetheart – let's get on with it.

(MURMURS OF PROTEST)

– 12 –

specimen layout for a radio play

Names of characters should be clearly separated from the speech and should be given in full throughout. Sound effects and other technical information should also be clearly differentiated from the speech. Directions indented, in full capitals and underlined. Although there are no scenes as such in a radio drama, the sequences in the sound picture should be indicated clearly, providing instructions regarding the transitions from one sound sequence to the next, for example CUT or FADE or Music (usually indicated as GRAMS in the script). Scene-sequences should be numbered as well as pages.

Exercise 35

Write the opening five minutes of a radio play. You may wish to experiment by trying to adapt a piece of your own writing or start afresh with a new idea.

Sending out your work

To the BBC

The New Writing Initiative states: 'Writers who previously had to guess where to submit their work now have a single address, and the confidence that, if their work is brilliant, it will be recommended to the right producers or development units across the BBC. We only recommend writers and scripts that have a strong chance of being commissioned. Please don't send scripts by email – we haven't the resources to print them up nor to assess them on screen.'

Attach a synopsis of the play together with a full cast list and brief notes on the main characters. Include a s.a.e. if you would like your script returned. Make sure it fits in the return envelope you provide. You can send your complete work by post to BBC The New Writing Co-ordinator at Room 222, BBC Broadcasting House, Portland Place, London W1A 1AA.

To an independent producer

As an alternative to the New Writing Initiative which will channel your work towards a suitable staff producer, you could approach an independent producer or production company. The BBC increasingly commissions work from independent sources. Send a synopsis of the play plus the opening ten minutes to give an initial flavour of the play, it's theme, style and characters etc. You will find a list of Independent Radio Producers in the *Writers' and Artists' Yearbook* which includes submission preferences.

Useful websites

BBC
For a wealth of helpful information for writers and more tips on how to get started visit the writers' section of the BBC website: www.bbc.co.uk/writersroom where you will find guidelines, interviews and a lively messageboard. Also included are further details of the BBC New Writing Initiative.

www.bbc.co.uk/worldservice/arts/features/howtowrite/ – The How To Write... section includes advice on the Radio Play.

IRDP
The website of the award winning Independent Radio Drama Productions is also well worth a visit. At www.irdp.co.uk/ you will find a step-by-step guide, hints, tips, history, links and resources – all radio drama related.

Australian Broadcasting Service Online
http://www.abc.net.au/classic/unborn/ Fascinating site which takes you from the idea for a radio drama right through to the broadcast. Based on Michael Cove's play *The Unborn*.

Oneword
A digital radio station available via Sky (channel 877) or on the internet www.oneword.co.uk Unlike most commercial radio stations which are music based, it's a spoken word channel and features books, drama, comedy and discussion.

stage and screen

In this chapter you will learn:
- how to get started writing drama for the stage
- the scope and challenge offered by television drama
- the differing script layouts for stage and screen.

The stage play

'You need three things in the theatre – the play, the actors and the audience, and each must give something' (Kenneth Haigh, in *Theatre Arts*, July 1958).

Let's paraphrase that Kenneth Haigh quote and use it as the basis for a quick tour of this huge subject. For our purpose, as writers, we'll substitute the word *actors* for *characters*.

The audience

We all know the delightful sense of anticipation we feel when we are waiting for a play to begin, the excitement when the lights go down and the curtain rises (if there *is* a curtain) on the first scene. The theatre-goer is eager to be entertained, having taken the trouble to make the journey, and your task as a playwright is to put yourself in his place and make sure that he feels a sense of involvement from the very beginning. You must constantly be aware of the need to keep him intrigued, whether your play is a thriller, a comedy or a drama.

The audience must be made to care at all times about what happens to the people on stage. As in a novel, there must be surprises combined with a sense of truth and inevitability.

The play

There is a great deal of sheer *craft* involved in writing for the theatre; you must be aware of the director, the actors, the stage and the audience as well as the structure of your play and the reality of your story.

Most plays deal with one main problem and you should start at a moment which heralds the first impact of that problem. The time and place must always be clear; there should really be no need for a programme to proclaim that it is 'Helen's bedroom' the next morning or 'Simon's study' three weeks later.

If you have introduced vital information in the first minutes of the play – in order to set up a twist ending perhaps – you will need to find other ways at later points in the play to 'sow the same seed'. It takes an audience time to 'get into' a play and it would be wrong to bury vital information too soon without finding an unobtrusive means to reiterate later.

Play lengths

The one-act play – most suitable of all for a first attempt – lasts from 30 to 45 minutes, but never longer than an hour. You should limit your cast to a maximum of six and concentrate on one dominant dramatic situation.

The three-act play – You may be wondering what an 'act' is in the context of a stage play. *Brewer's Theatre* (Cassell) defines it as '…one of the major structural divisions of a play. The end of an act, which can contain several scenes, is often indicated by the lowering of the curtain or by raising the house lights.' It often coincides with a jump in time.

The modern play is often not divided into three acts, two is more common now with a single interval. The trend is for shorter plays, approximately two hours in length. The duration of the interval will be decided by the theatre management. The second act is usually shorter than the first. At this length one or two sub-plots may be included (provided they are related to the main theme) and there is time for a more gradual development.

Whatever the length, plays, perhaps more than any other form of fiction, need convincing and exciting characterization.

The characters

The actors will obviously interpret and bring to life the characters you create but they cannot do it *unless you give them the words.* Establish your characters in good time so that members of the audience don't have to whisper to one another, 'Who's that – his wife or his sister?' Allow your characters to express their feelings strongly, not only in words but in actions; emotions will run high from time to time. (Successful playwrights are not usually hampered by inhibitions!)

In a full length play you might have up to ten characters but a smaller cast is easier to handle when you are inexperienced, quite apart from the cost of production.

Dialogue and character motivation

Consider every aspect of the dialogue, not only what the people say but how much they say, (and how little) how they say it and to whom they talk most easily and honestly. We all know how certain people encourage communication and others block it. The blocking of communication is one of the greatest causes of conflict in a play (as in real life) and you must use your skills to build up tension in your audience through the clash of personalities as well as through the action itself.

In general, keep speeches fairly short (there will, of course, be exceptions) and remember that people have a habit of interrupting one another especially when they are angry or distressed. Avoid 'party chatter' and 'charlady chatter'; it may be amusing but if it doesn't contribute to the development of the story it has no place in your play. One of the secrets is to watch out for any passages of inessential dialogue and ruthlessly prune them away. If a word/phrase/speech can be dispensed with and still leave the scene intact, then it must go.

Beware of feeding information to the audience in an obvious way, making your characters tell each other things they know perfectly well already ('After all, I'm your son.' 'We've only been here since Friday.'). One way of overcoming this problem is to introduce a newcomer who, like the audience, has to know who's who and what's going on.

Learning the craft

Writing is a problem-solving occupation. No matter which new project you embark on, no matter which form or genre you choose, you will probably encounter problems. They are usually best dealt with one at a time so the best way to learn how to deal with them is to start the 'journey' and take each as it comes.

To write well for the stage you must know the stage. So go to the theatre; support your local theatre and amateur dramatic groups. See as many plays as you can and choose a wide variety – experimental and traditional – and look at them all with a writer's eye. Take a notebook. Can you imagine a journalist or an article writer going to an event without pen and paper?

Research

As your theatre research file builds up it will help you to remember the different techniques employed in the plays you have seen. Attending a local theatre is inexpensive and above all enjoyable. Enjoy the play while it's happening but jot down the answers to the following questions as soon as you get home:

1 What *form* did the play take – how many acts and how many scenes per act?
2 What shape did the story have – where did the author choose to begin the story, how did this develop and how did the story end?
3 How many characters were there?
4 Where and when was the play set?
5 How many different sets were used?
6 How much dialogue was used?
7 How often was there no dialogue at all – and what was happening?
8 What were the high points of the play, for example, the highest points of tension and suspense?
9 What was the problem or source of conflict?
10 In what ways did the conflict affect the characters individually?
11 How long was the play (not counting the interval)?
12 What was the theme of the play?

Join a dramatic society if you can; this will help you to get in touch with the mechanics of the theatre and avoid the mistakes so often made by new writers. You will learn how to organize changes of scene if you need them, how to get your characters on and off stage and how to write dialogue which is *speakable*. You will make sure that even the smallest part is vital and interesting to play and you will allow time for the actors to change their costumes if necessary between appearances. These things may seem obvious but you'd be surprised how many beginners forget them.

Keep your stage directions to the bare essentials. That's the director's job and the author should bow to his wishes as far as possible. Remember that your play is much more likely to be accepted if it is not expensive to produce, so avoid period costume, large casts and elaborate sets. The real quality of a play depends upon *character* and *suspense*.

In addition to your 'live' theatre researches, read as many plays as you can, both old and new; there is normally a good selection in the public libraries.

The following plays would form a good basis for study: *All My Sons* by Arthur Miller; *The Norman Conquests* by Alan Ayckbourn; *Look Back in Anger* by John Osborne; *The Caretaker* by Harold Pinter; *Abigail's Party* by Mike Leigh; and *Rosencrantz and Guildenstern Are Dead* by Tom Stoppard.

What are your chances?

There is a certain magic associated with the theatre more than any other medium. If your ideas are all channelled towards the stage and your urge to write always leads you to the stage – then you're hooked and you will write in this medium no matter what. It's very difficult to make money in this field but if you choose to experiment creatively you will be rewarded with a wealth of learning and understanding which will stand you in good stead in other forms of writing.

Script layout

The recommended layout for a script is as follows:

1 Character's names are shown on the left of the page.
2 Dialogue is shown in normal upper and lower case and should be single spaced.
3 Leave a blank line after each speech or direction.
4 Stage directions are shown all in capitals and single spaced. A direction to the actor is shown in normal case and enclosed in brackets after the character's name.
5 Give directions sparingly. The dialogue should speak for itself. Stage directions should convey essential information only.
6 Provide a synopsis of the play plus a brief thumbnail sketch of each character.

See page 156.

Further reading

Faber Critical Guides: Tom Stoppard by Jim Hunter (Faber).

The Playwright's Process: Learning the Craft from Today's Leading Dramatists by Buzz McLaughlin (Back Stage Books).

Perfect 10: Writing and Producing the 10-Minute Play by Gary Garrison (Heinemann).

The *Writers' and Artists' Yearbook* or *The Writer's Handbook* will help you to track down publishers, small presses, competitions, magazines and production companies.

Useful website

To find out where your nearest theatre is in the UK visit the theatre website directory: www.thisisbritishtheatre.co.uk This site will provide the address and contact number of your

ACT ONE. SCENE TWO (continued)

MAURICE (Angrily) You'd better get on the phone and cancel that
         booking this minute.

ANN   But I need a holiday – I'll have a nervous breakdown if
         I don't get away –

MAURICE If you cancel now there won't be anything to pay –

ANN   Pay! Pay! All you think about is money –

MAURICE Pick up that phone!

ANN   You don't *listen* to me – you've *never* listened to me –

MAURICE Are you going to phone the agency and cancel that booking?

                 ANN SHAKES HER HEAD AND COVERS
                 HER FACE WITH HER HANDS.

MAURICE All right – I'll phone them myself.

                 HE GOES TO THE PHONE AND LOOKS IN
                 THE BOOK FOR THE NUMBER.

                 ANN RUNS TO HIM AND GRABS HIS
                 ARM.

ANN   (Hysterically) No – Maurice – please! I've bought some new
         things specially for the holiday – *please* –

MAURICE With whose money?

ANN   Mine, of course – that mother left me –

                 MAURICE PUSHES HER AWAY FROM HIM AND
                 ANN COLLAPSES ON TO THE SETTEE.

                 DAVID COMES IN FROM THE KITCHEN, DRINKING
                 BEER.

DAVID   (Coldly) At it again, you two? Mum, where's my blue
         blazer?

ANN   (Calming down) It's at the cleaners. It'll be back tomorrow.

20

specimen layout for a stage play

nearest theatre and provide a link, where available, which will take you to its website. It promises that your local theatre's site will also provide local information on where to eat and drink. Happy researching!

Exercise 36

Write the opening five minutes of a one act play together with story synopsis and details of characters.

Television drama

It would be misleading for me to imply that a novice might 'teach himself' to write television drama from just part of a chapter in a book such as this but I hope this section will set you off in the right direction.

Getting started

The door is open to anyone with special talent who can master the techniques required. As with all other forms of drama, it is the strength of the theme, the characterization and the story line which will alert a producer to your potential. And if you can turn out a piece of work which is not only well written but also shines out as genuinely *different* you may well see your play produced on the small screen even though you are comparatively inexperienced. An original approach is perhaps the most valuable asset any writer has to offer.

We are all familiar with television as consumers but putting yourself 'behind the camera' will reveal an array of techniques which will be unfamiliar at first. You will need to think visually, to break the story down into scenes, to use story strands or sub-plots and to structure the story in order to produce pace and variety.

There's no need to worry too much about the technicalities of production and camera work, although later on an understanding of what goes on in studio and on location will help.

A first project in television

Exercise 37

To familiarize yourself with TV writing techniques, take a short story of your own and attempt to adapt it for television. You should do this without thought of the length or the market or of submitting it anywhere but simply to discover what changes would need to be made in order to make it work on television. If, at this stage, you find you do not have a story suitable for adaptation then why not choose a favourite, published short story to see whether or not it could work for television. By using an existing story the plot and characterization are already established allowing you to concentrate solely on the new medium you are working in.

You may soon become aware that not all stories *can* make the transition from page to screen.

Acclaimed screenwriter William Goldman, in his highly anecdotal and yet practical book, *Adventures in the Screentrade* (Abacus), gives himself the task of taking one of his early short stories, *Da Vinci* (3,500 words approximately) and turning it into a screenplay. Mr Goldman's screenwriting credits include *Butch Cassidy and the Sundance Kid*, *All the President's Men*, *Marathon Man*, *A Bridge Too Far*, *The Stepford Wives*, *Misery* and *Fierce Creatures*. You can follow his thought processes through three chapters as he overcomes the problems encountered. Along the way he asks some basic questions: What's The Story About? What's The Story *Really* About? What About Time? Who Tells The Story? Where Does The Story Take Place? What About The Characters? What Must We Cling To?

Whilst I am not suggesting that television and film are the same, there are areas of common ground which can provide you with a glimpse of both media, enough to get you started. As you begin the process you will quickly realize that all of the descriptive passages in the story can now be *shown* and they take up very little screen or story time.

The story, the characters and the dialogue are now emphasized and dialogue takes on a different role. You may find that *less* dialogue is needed as so much more can be shown to the audience by other visual means, not least the wordless skills of the actors. It's a fascinating process and one which will teach you much about both the story and the 'film'.

If you undertake this exercise and discover you have leanings in this direction, I suggest that you read one or two textbooks on the subject whilst trying to develop an original script of your own. There are respected screenwriting courses and qualifications as well as script workshops which would help you on your way.

Research

The video recorder enables you to go back over a drama many times to isolate a sequence of scenes for further study and to analyse the composition and structure of the story.

Here is an nine point checklist:

1 How many scenes are there?
2 How long is each scene? (You may need a stopwatch!)
3 What does each scene achieve, that is, how does it move the story forwards?
4 How many different storylines or sub plots are there?
5 What role does dialogue play – is it prominent or sparse?
6 How is suspense established and maintained?
7 How many interior and exterior scenes were used?
8 What was the theme?
9 What is the source of conflict and how does it affect the characters?

It will help your understanding of television/film writing if you can obtain a final script and watch the final production with reference to it. Complete scripts are available in book form, so check with your local bookshop, library or favourite online book shop. For example, the screenplay for *Four Weddings and a Funeral* by Richard Curtis is published by Corgi Books and provides the complete script as well as scenes which didn't make it to the screen.

Short films for television

Films made for television, ranging from ten to 15 minutes in length can offer a good start point. FilmFour showcases new talent via *The Shooting Gallery*, a collection of varied and original short films, some highly experimental. To discover more visit www.filmfour.com The website will tell you if they are commissioning at the moment or give an indication when they will be in the future.

Television plays

Single plays may last for 75 to 90 minutes and offer the best opening for a novice – however this is almost like saying that it would be better to start your climbing career with the Eiger rather than Everest!

The serial presents a continuous narrative, each episode ending on a note of suspense and building towards a final episode.

The series consists of several plays written around the same theme/characters, each one complete in itself. Many series also have a strong serial theme running through them, that is, they can only be transmitted in a given order of episodes.

Roy Russell, author of many successful television drama scripts, has this valuable advice to offer: 'A commercially oriented play is one that has a strong story and fascinating characters. Series episodes are really plays, and their entertainment value is heightened not diminished if the writer is also trying to make an underlying point intrinsic to the story and the characters.'

The writing of an individual episode for a series or a serial is not usually associated with the beginner. Here are a few general tips for writing a single play.

Tips

Be economical in your settings. Remember, also, to be economical with your characters. As with stage and radio drama, a real person must now be employed (and paid) to recreate character. Characters must give good value.

Don't ask for a large elaborate set for one short scene. If you want a palatial drawing room with chandeliers and fabulous furnishings let most of your action take place there. When scenes are shot on location they are not only costly to produce but demand special writing techniques.

You would be wise to make a careful study of one or more of the textbooks available before you plan your play.

Further reading

Writing for Television by Gerald Kelsey (A. & C. Black).

Writing for Television by William Smethhurst (How To Books).

Adventures in the Screentrade by William Goldman (Abacus).

Script layout

1 Plays for television require a special layout. On the title page you must state the running time, carefully estimated by reading it aloud and allowing for pauses and actions. As a very rough guide only, an A4 page of dialogue will play between a minute and a minute-and-a-half, but a page of short speeches will obviously play faster than one with a couple of long speeches, owing to the layout.

2 Isolate the names of the characters in a separate column, using capital letters and typing each name *in full* throughout the script. Initials or abbreviations are not acceptable as they are confusing to anyone who has not read the play before.

3 The speeches should be in single spacing with double spacing between. The important thing is that the words to be spoken should stand out unmistakably.

4 When you type a television play, as you will see in the figure, you must only use the right-hand half of the page. The left-hand half is for camera instructions and need not concern you.

5 Don't be intimidated by the techniques; it's the story and the characters that count. Nevertheless, you should, as always, take care to present your work in a professional manner.

Here is some advice from the BBC:-

'If you are sending your work to the BBC as part of the New Writing Initiative here are a few submission guidelines:

Apart from a full length script – 75–90 minutes running time, your submission should also include (on no more than 2 sides of A4 paper):

Up to two lines with the title and genre of the piece, including when and where the play is set.

One or two paragraphs on the subject matter of your play.

A maximum 1 page synopsis (3–5 paragraphs preferred) describing the major events in your play.'

Send to: Films and Single Drama, Jessica Dromgoole, New Writing Co-ordinator, Room 222, BBC Broadcasting House, Portland Place, London W1A 1AA. Tel: 020 7765 0756. Unsolicited scripts can still be sent to individual producers in London and the regions but this is likely to take longer due to individual workloads.

SC3.   INT   LIVING ROOM   DAY

[THE ROOM IS QUITE SMALL,
COMFORTABLE, CHEAPLY
FURNISHED, UNTIDY. IVY'S
SISTER JOSIE IS SITTING ON THE
FLOOR, SEWING A LONG SKIRT.
SHE IS OLDER THAN IVY, THIN,
SERIOUS, RATHER MASCULINE.
IVY IS LYING ON THE SOFA WITH
HER SHOES OFF, EATING
CHOCOLATE].

IVY: I still can't see why she didn't *tell* me. It
always comes back to that, doesn't it?

JOSIE: She'll have her reasons. Why must you
always nose into people's affairs?

IVY: But I used to be sort of engaged to him. I
must have told you – tall with flaming hair.
His father was a doctor. Don't you *remember*?

JOSIE: Of course I don't remember – it's
donkey's years ago. Why do you always expect
me to remember your things? You don't
remember mine.

[IVY IGNORES THIS; SHE IS SLOW
TO TAKE OFFENCE]

IVY: I can't see why Mandy didn't tell me.
I'd have thought she'd be proud of it, marrying
Dennis Fogg. He was a real dish. Though I must
say he frightened us all to death with his guns.

JOSIE: [LOOKING UP IN ALARM] *Guns?*

IVY: He was mad about air guns – always
shooting birds and rabbits. I hated that, of course,
but he was a crack shot. Won masses of things
at fairs. Once he tried to make poor Mandy
let him shoot an apple off her head. She was
terrified.

– 15 –

specimen layout for a television play

Synopsis example:

Martin Roberts, 55, is awakened in the middle of the night by a phone call from his estranged wife, Laura, who left him five years earlier for another man. She says she is phoning from a local call box and will be with him in a few minutes. He has never ceased to love her and ... etc.

Details of the BBC's New Writing Initiative can be found on their web page: www.bbc.co.uk/writersroom where you will find full details including useful addresses.

Exercise 38

Write the first five minutes (carefully timed) of a television play, together with a brief synopsis of the story, a list of characters and the sets/locations involved in the story.

the non-fiction book

In this chapter you will learn:
- how to 'test' your idea for a full length book
- the importance of researching your subject and the market
- how and when to approach a publisher.

As we have seen in Chapter 3, How to Write an Article, it is 'easier' to place an article with a magazine than it is a short story. The same holds true when comparing the prospects for a non-fiction book with those of the novel.

When you walk into a large bookshop a vast array of titles compete for your attention. Books on child care, bee-keeping, sailing, yoga, calligraphy, how to reduce junk mail, start a business, upgrade a computer, make a complaint, and much more are all ranged before you.

A book is rarely a success unless the author is spurred on by real enthusiasm for the subject and can back this up with knowledge, experience and expertise. For instance, you wouldn't dream of attempting a cookery book unless you had been a dedicated cook for many years. It is, in my view, a mistake to 'mug-up' a subject from scratch in order to write about it. You might succeed in this way with a short article but the writing of a full-length book requires a solid background of knowledge and a deep commitment.

Does your non-fiction idea warrant a book?

Let's assume you have an idea which excites you but you're not quite sure if it will sustain the length of a book. How do you avoid finding yourself stranded less than half way with all of your material used up?

You could start by considering, even at this tentative stage, how you might approach a publisher. This may seem odd, but if you can answer the kinds of questions the publisher would eventually ask, you could save yourself a lot of work and clarify your thoughts at the same time.

In the field of non-fiction it is unusual to write the whole book and then try to sell it to a publisher. After a period of market research, planning and research an author would approach a publisher with a package comprising a covering letter, a book proposal and a detailed synopsis including the Contents list. Let's concentrate first on the book proposal.

What is a book proposal?

Its purpose is to sell the project to the publisher, stimulate interest and prove the market potential of the idea. He would almost certainly want to have an input early on – *before* the whole book is written. But, at this stage, you must prove the idea's worth to *your* satisfaction.

So let's go through the questions a book proposal should answer, as it will help you to determine whether or not you have a viable project in mind.

What is the book about?

Books are seldom about subjects in their entirety. They usually focus on a single aspect offering a fresh insight or a new angle on a particular facet of the subject. With this in mind, break down your chosen subject into a series of topic headings. Jot them down until you find the area which excites you most and makes the most of your knowledge and experience. Later, if you decide to go ahead with the project, you will need to capture the essence of the book in just one or two sentences in your presentation to the publisher.

Why should it be published?

What would the reader gain from buying this book? Decide who your reader would be – a beginner, completely new to the subject or someone who is already proficient and wants to broaden existing knowledge? Is there a wave of new interest in the subject? What new angle are you bringing to the topic?

Chapter breakdown

Work out a rough list of chapter headings and arrange them in the best possible order. This will form your Contents list and requires a great deal of consideration. I had some difficulty when I was planning this book in deciding, for instance, whether to place 'Characterization' before or after 'The Short Story'. I decided eventually, as you have seen, to put 'The Short Story' first. It seemed appropriate to discuss construction (the bones) before characterization (the flesh). However, you may think that I was wrong, bearing in mind that character is usually the most important aspect of a story. Put yourself in the reader's place, picturing his difficulties and arranging your information in the most helpful way. Never forget that trial and error are part of the task; the book will have to remain in a fluid state until the last draft – which may be the fifth or sixth.

A good tip is to write each chapter heading on a separate piece of paper without numbering them so you can easily experiment with the order. Add sub-headings on each chapter's page as they occur to you. Make rough estimates of how many words each chapter would need. Later, this breakdown may form the basis for your synopsis but in the meantime it will help to give your idea form and shape.

How many pages?

Using your rough outline you can now estimate how many words the book is likely to be. The answer to this question will be crucial. Non-fiction books generally range from 30,000 words upwards. If you think your idea will fall a long way short of this minimum then you will either need to find more material or accept that your idea might be better as the basis for a series of articles. Collaboration might be an option – see the section below. Consideration of other books in this subject area might be helpful at this stage.

Who are the competition?

A trip to the book shop, or the book shop's website, is always worthwhile. Take a notepad and pencil and head for the department which has books in your subject area. Note down titles, authors and publishers. How many printed pages do they have? A printed page of text is, say, 350 to 400 words. You can quickly estimate roughly how many words there are.

If no book exists on your chosen theme, then your lucky stars are shining and you must be sure to plan the book so carefully and write it so well that no publisher could refuse it.

Look at the various approaches the authors have adopted – the arrangement of chapters and sub-headings. Note the use of illustrations and diagrams. This might inspire a fresh approach for your book. Make a list of the publishers and look them up later in the *Writers' and Artists' Yearbook* or *The Writer's Handbook*. What unique advantages would your book have over the others?

If there are several books in print already, can you identify an aspect of the subject not covered? Do you think you could adapt your idea to fill that gap? You may realize that you can fill a niche here, cover a missing area, bring the topic up to date perhaps and add a new angle. If there are several books in print – and you should read as many as you can – it is essential that your book has something new and original to offer.

Choosing a publisher

Your initial researches at the bookshop will have identified a number of publishers in this field. Follow this up by referring to the *Writers' and Artists' Yearbook* or *The Writer's Handbook*, paying particular attention to their submission requirements – how many sample chapters they require and the format of the submission. Visit the website if there is one. Send for (or download) guidelines if they are available. Write off for current catalogues. Make your choice. Consider publishers who produce the *type* of book you are considering but have nothing in your exact topic area. You may have identified a gap in their range of topics.

Query letter

If you have proved to yourself that you have a viable project in mind it's a good time to narrow your choice of publishers down to a short list then select the most suitable. You can now write a brief, positive letter which tells the publisher what the book is about, the proposed length, how you think it will fit into his list, etc. Include a little about yourself, for example, relevant experience but keep the letter to a single page if possible. You should say that you would be prepared to write sample chapters if he is interested.

And now wait.

You will probably get a prompt reply. If you are not successful send a fresh query letter to the next publisher on the list.

Writing sample chapters

If a publisher writes back expressing an interest he will probably ask you to prepare a book proposal and sample chapters – without commitment on his part. Now is the time to decide in much greater detail on the construction of a sample chapter or two. Finalize the headings, gather material, make notes – and start to write. Update your knowledge, check all the facts, research further into the latest developments. Keep your attention focussed on just these two chapters. Inevitably you'll discover many things outside your current area of focus, but save surplus material until later and concentrate solely on your topic. It's a good idea right from the start to keep organized notes. Develop a file structure of information so you always know where to find it later. But above all, don't allow yourself to be distracted from your two chapters. Write, re-write, edit and polish until you feel they are as good as they can be.

Work schedule

The time it takes you to write the sample chapters will provide a good gauge when deciding how much time you will need to write the whole book. You can now go back to your original 'book proposal' and re-write it in the light of all you have learned, tailoring your submission to the requirements of your chosen publisher.

Further information you will need to add to your proposal will include:

Personal details

Give details of your current occupation, and writing track-record so far (if any) and send photocopies of magazine articles you've had published (if possible) – even if they are not on the same subject.

Your expertise in this field

Give full details of your experience and expertise in this field together with the extent of your researches.

Your proposed deadline

Don't create problems for yourself later by setting this date too heroically tight.

Any special presentation features required

Give an indication of the use of drawings, photographs, graphs, diagrams, etc.

Promotion of the book

Include anything relevant which you could do to help promote the book, for example, if you are a member of a society or association connected with the subject you should mention this.

Foreign sales potential?

Would there be additional markets overseas?

Bringing the package together

You now have two chapters and a proposal but you must add to this a synopsis of the book – a chapter-by-chapter breakdown including sub-headings with a brief description of each.

Remember, you may be putting your idea up against others being proposed at the same time and it is the job of your 'package' to capture the publisher's attention and imagination proving to him that this is the project to proceed with. It convinced you, now it must convince him!

Your covering letter

The covering letter is probably the last part of the package you write and, very importantly, it is the first thing the publisher will read. It is, therefore, not something to be dashed off without thought. It should be professional and confident in tone without trace of 'hype' or arrogance. Remind the publisher of his earlier interest in the project.

Enclosures

Make sure it is clear in your letter exactly what you have submitted. It is essential to include return postage and suitable return envelope/packaging.

Your covering letter should be a single page only. Your proposal should be no more than a single page. And the chapter-by-chapter synopsis should be 2–3 pages at the most, single spaced.

What are your chances?

Your submission package will provide a good impression of the book you have in mind. Any changes you make subsequently (for example, additional chapters or the rearrangement of those already listed) will not substantially affect the book – except to improve it.

If it turns out that the publisher is not interested after all then you must resume your quest. Always take heed of comments made by a publisher in turning a project down and be prepared to be flexible.

Commissions

An unknown author might well obtain a commission for such a book if the subject is suitable and the standard of writing in the specimen chapters satisfactory. Anyone who is successful with articles should find no problem.

My husband, Stanley, proved this point by receiving a contract from Gollancz (now a member of the Orion Publishing Group) to write his book *Make Your Own Classical Guitar.* Previously he had written only articles, but a similar book did not exist, he had expert knowledge of the subject and Gollancz were wise enough to recognize the potential of a DIY book which would be likely to sell steadily for many years.

Don't be discouraged if the first few publishers you try aren't interested. I think Gollancz was number seven on Stanley's list.

Collaboration

Striking up a writing partnership with a trusted friend, as I did with Kay Horowicz to produce *Fun With Stamps* (see Chapter 16), is one thing but not all writing collaborations begin from such a firm base. What if you are faced with the prospect of writing in partnership with a colleague or an acquaintance? Here are a few of the pros and cons which you should consider before entering into an agreement. I will start with the cons first. These need far greater consideration than the pros!

Cons

- Division of workload is not always easy. It might be that the most natural division isn't fair and a greater burden falls on one rather than the other.
- Overall responsibility for the project can become blurred. Who has the final say? Who deals with the publisher or the agent?
- Consultation process between partners can take up time before agreement is reached.
- There is certainly a need for a written agreement – but it is difficult for any agreement to cover all things in all circumstances.
- Expenses can cause problems, who paid for what, who claims for what?

Pros

- If your prospective partner has a different but complementary knowledge from your own this would broaden and enhance the scope of the book.

- Working in partnership provides stimulation – ideas can emerge from brainstorming sessions, problems can be solved through discussion.
- If the partnership is 'right' the weaknesses of one can be compensated for by the strengths of the other.
- Areas of research can be shared helping to cut down the time involved.
- Partnership deadlines can help to keep the book on schedule – regular meetings, dispatching work by email by agreed times, etc.
- Critical feedback helps to keep things on track.

Collaboration is not something to be entered into lightly of course and it needs a lot of thought before a commitment is made – samples of work exchanged, meetings and discussions held. But if the circumstances are right, and the partner is right, it can be a positive arrangement for both.

Travel books

There's a big difference between a 'traveller' and a 'tourist' and it's one which divides the Travel book section into two. A 'traveller' is probably willing to do without home comforts whilst exploring a country and getting to know its people. A travel writer in this part of the divide is writing not only for the fellow traveller who might like to follow in his footsteps but for the armchair traveller who wants to experience the journey vicariously – to be taken there by the power and sometimes the poetry of the narrative. A tourist wants a more practical view of the country, the places to visit, where to stay, costs, places of entertainment, tours, etc. Each writer takes a different angle on the subject and caters for a different market.

To give you an idea of the level of interest in travel and travel writing, Lonely Planet produce over 400 guidebooks, phrase books, walking guides, atlases, city maps, videos and travel literature titles. Nearly one million people *per month* visit the Lonely Planet website (www.lonelyplanet.com) Amazon have a searchable database of 49,000 titles in the Travel and Holiday category alone (this includes maps and atlases, etc).

It's a big field and a very tough market. The principles of writing hold as good for the travel writing sector as in any other. Know your reader, study the market, pay attention to the construction of the piece and adopt a fresh approach. Study the books you admire, not so that you can imitate them but so that you may differ from them.

Whatever approach you decide to adopt, you must *know* the place you propose to write about. Planning your chapters is, once again, the best way to start. Don't make the mistake of including too many details; when you know your subject very well, there is a great temptation to overload your book, making it indigestible.

Your job is to select unusual and interesting facts, to discard those which do not fit into the scheme of your book, and to use the others with flair and charm. Don't forget that not all travel writing is international and global. There are small press printers locally who might be interested in a book on, say, Pub Walks in Warwickshire or 25 Short Walks Starting From Your Car.

Biography and autobiography

A biography is an account of someone's life story and is said to be 'authorized' if it is written by someone approved of by that person or his descendants, etc. An unauthorized biography is written without the permission or approval of the subject. An autobiography on the other hand is a life story written by the person himself. I will concentrate on the autobiography as this is more likely to be an appealing project to a novice.

Successful autobiographies are usually written by people who have done something of outstanding significance. In a recent spot check at the book shop I counted a total of 350 biographies and autobiographies on sale side by side. Twenty-five of the books (about seven per cent) were by 'ordinary' people. Among them were: – a schools inspector from Yorkshire; a Vietnam veteran; an abused child; a climber; a Lancashire family's history; a reformed football hooligan and a person addicted to reading books.

Many of my students have told me about their exciting lives – teaching in Africa, serving as air-raid wardens in the London blitz, going on cruises around the world – hoping that I would encourage them to write their autobiographies. I hate to have to tell them that hundreds of people have done these things and that it requires a very special talent to write a publishable book on experiences which, although they are of great significance to the person concerned, are not sufficiently outstanding. Perhaps you have that special talent; if so let nothing deter you.

In any case, your rich experiences will provide material for articles. Another possibility is to use them as background in a novel. Many famous writers have utilized their travels in this way – notably Somerset Maugham, H. E. Bates, Graham Greene and Paul Scott. In such cases you create a fictitious story and imaginary characters; on no account be tempted to put *yourself* into the novel, merely disguising your identity by changing your name! It is a grave mistake, in almost every case, to put real people into fiction.

You may feel that you would like to write the story of your life for the benefit of your children and grandchildren. This, of course, is a delightful enterprise, so long as you have no expectations of getting it published. However, it will be much more satisfying to you – and to your readers – if the book is well planned and well written. Beware of including too many trivial incidents and personal opinions. Select the most significant aspects of your life and write them up in a lively style, dividing the book into chapters of not more than 2500 words. Sometimes a novice will continue without a break – even without a new paragraph – for 30 pages or so. No grandchild would ever stay the course!

Presentation of manuscripts

Books should be typed in the same way as short stories (double spacing on good quality A4 paper, with generous margins, etc.) but serial rights do not apply and your title sheet must bear no reference to them. When you sell a book, the terms are stated in a publisher's contract which you will sign when the negotiations are completed.

If you need to add material after your book is typed you may number additional pages 37A, 37B and so on – but don't do it too often! If your book includes charts and diagrams figure numbers should relate to each chapter separately rather than run continuously through the book. Remember, also, to weight headings according to their importance – upper case for main headings, lower-case bold for sub-headings, etc.

There is no need to bind your typescript, though you may hold the pages of each chapter together with paper clips. Most publishers prefer loose pages so they can easily be separated (the editor might wish to put part of your book in his briefcase to read on the train).

Every publisher's dream is to discover a brilliant new author, and your manuscript will certainly be studied with care and interest. This does not mean that all full typescripts are read from beginning to end. A professional reader can discern from the first few pages whether or not a book is likely to be publishable.

You should attach a self-addressed label bearing the correct postage for its return if unsuitable and remember to keep a copy of your manuscript.

Send your 'sales package' off and be prepared to wait for a decision. During that time do not write, telephone or email and *on no account* pay a personal visit. Try to forget the book and get on with the next one, although your heart will probably jump every time the post is delivered.

Exercise 39

If you have an idea for a non-fiction book use this chapter as a step-by-step guide to evaluate the strengths and weakness of the project.

part four

the technical side

of writing

20

the writing fraternity

In this chapter you will learn:
- the benefits of joining a writers' circle
- how to make contact with fellow writers locally and nationally
- where to find creative writing courses and writers' conferences.

Creative writing classes

Writing can be a lonely occupation and although non-writing friends and relatives may be willing to 'help' there's no substitute for feedback from a fellow writer. If you are just starting out, I can recommend creative writing classes, especially those run by local education authorities. These offer low cost courses with qualified tutors and can be an inspiration as well as an education. However, not every area offers writing as a subject. Your local library will be able to help with further information.

Writing conferences

Annual conferences usually include lectures, workshops and discussion groups as well as tremendous social interaction and they offer a great boost. Valuable friendships are formed at mealtimes and in the bar. I have found, after attending such conferences for many years, that the writing fraternity is wonderfully generous in sharing experience and offering advice. A list of well-known conferences is included at the end of this chapter.

Joining a writers' circle

Perhaps the answer for you is to join a writers' circle. Most can boast a few experts but in any case you will learn a lot from other amateurs; a fresh eye can often spot mistakes in your manuscript you have overlooked. For anyone who is not afraid of criticism, a local group can be the beginning of success. It was for me.

Enquire at your local library to find out if there is a writers' circle near you. Most circles will allow prospective new members to sit in so you can decide if the group will be right for you. (See Useful websites and addresses later on in this chapter.)

What to look for in a writers' circle

Frequency of meetings

If it's feedback you need, a circle meeting only once a month may not be suitable. Twelve meetings per year will obviously be limiting. Fortnightly meetings are a good compromise, though some circles meet every week.

There should be a definite time to start with people gathering, say, 15 minutes earlier for a warming-up chat but, once the meeting has begun, the group should concentrate entirely on writing matters. If possible the group should keep going throughout the year without a break; summer recesses can ruin good resolutions. Meetings should be at least two hours in duration.

Venue

I think it is better if the group does not meet in each other's houses. This has the disadvantage of encouraging chit-chat rather than serious work. Curtains are admired, photographs passed around and recipes exchanged; small wonder that male writers sometimes decide that a circle is not for them!

Another argument against meeting in private houses is that it provokes competition over the standard of refreshments provided. It may also cause embarrassment to those who, for one reason or another, are unable to provide hospitality. Wherever the meeting is held, the group should be a working rather than a social group.

Feedback

On your first visit, try to gauge the particular strengths of the circle. If the majority of members seem to be novelists or playwrights, it might not be suitable for you if your subject area is, say, non-fiction or poetry. A good cross-section of writing topics is a healthy sign.

Each meeting should allow plenty of time for manuscripts to be read and comments obtained. A reasonable reading time should be allowed for each member who wants to read but this should not be limitless! A set reading time or an agreed number of words is best, not least because listening to a piece of work with a view to offering criticism demands great concentration.

The chairman should ensure that comments provoke discussion on the quality of the writing, not on the subject matter, otherwise an article on blood sports, for example, might create bad feeling. A happy atmosphere is vital if the group is to thrive.

Criticism should be detailed and outspoken but never discouraging. It should be on as deep a level as possible with special attention to construction. Possible markets should be suggested if the work is considered saleable. We all feel sensitive about our work but those who are nervous of criticism often grow braver when they see other members accepting it gratefully, acting upon it and selling their work as a result.

Some circles organize internal competitions with set themes but if these are *too* frequent the reading out of winning entries and runners-up can regularly restrict the amount of time available to spend on manuscripts.

Many groups have members ranging from 18 to 80 and beyond. I know a lady who sold her first article at the age of 76. She had been wise enough to profit from the advice of fellow writers.

Group organization

As a visitor you should be welcomed by someone who has been given the job of host or hostess to ensure that you feel at ease and can find out all the things you want to know. In my view, anyone with a sincere desire to improve his or her work should be eligible to join. Publication ought never to be a condition of membership because writers' circles exist to help people into print. Nobody who works hard and welcomes criticism should feel unworthy to belong. There are many unpublished manuscripts of great merit and many published ones of little merit. Originality, enthusiasm and perseverance are the qualities I most admire in the members of my group, irrespective of commercial success. In any case, today's unpublished writers can be the bestsellers of tomorrow.

The subscription

The annual fee should be as low as possible. It is quite common for there to be an additional small contribution for each session attended to build up funds for professional speakers, competition prizes, social events and so on.

Fringe benefits

A magazine swap table can help to cut down the cost of market research by making available *recent* copies to other members. A scrapbook containing press cuttings on writing topics and a small library of books on writing can be made available to members. News of writing competitions helps to keep members informed of opportunities.

What about the internet?

Yes, there are 'writers' groups' and 'communities' on the internet where writers can 'meet', review one another's work, pass on tips, exchange news, gossip and perhaps sometimes share a few of the frustrations of writing. There are many first rate 'communities' and if you are online you may want to try them. However, no matter how good they are, what they don't do is get you out of the house, they don't get you away from the computer screen and they are all at the mercy of technology which can go wrong at any time, especially in a global context. So, be cautious and view the internet writers' circle as a useful addition to your available resources but not a substitute for interaction.

Useful websites and addresses

The Writers' Circles Handbook includes the regularly updated *Directory of Writers Circles*. Contact Jill Dick at Oldacre, Chapel-on-le-Frith, High Peak, Derbyshire SK23 9SY. www.cix.co.uk/~oldacre/ email: jillie@cix.co.uk

National Association of Writers Groups (NAWG) www.nawg.co.uk/ You can email the Secretary, Diane Wilson, on mikediane@tesco.net for further information.

www.author.co.uk/circles includes a section on UK writers' circles arranged by region and giving contacts, etc.

Courses and conferences

There are many creative writing courses available throughout the UK. Here are a few of the most well known:

The well-known **Arvon Foundation** offers courses for any serious student, regardless of previous experience. Grants and bursaries are available for those on low incomes. Subjects covered include poetry, fiction, stage drama, writing for TV and radio and writing for children. Their three residential centres are:

Totleigh Barton, Sheepwash, Beaworthy, Devon EX21 5NS.
email: t-barton@arvonfoundation.org

Lumb Bank, Heptonstall, Hebden Bridge, West Yorkshire HX7 6DF.
email: l-bank@arvonfoundation.org

Moniack Mhor, Teavarran, Kiltarlity, Beauly, Inverness-shire IV4 7HT.
email: m-mhor@arvonfoundation.org

Or visit the Arvon Foundation Website: www.arvonfoundation.org

I have taught at Totleigh Barton and can promise a very enjoyable and rewarding five days. A group of up to 16 aspiring writers works closely with the tutor in a peaceful setting, and the atmosphere is friendly and informal. Work is assessed carefully and the students are given detailed and constructive criticism by a professional tutor. The accommodation is comfortable but not luxurious and the students take turns in preparing meals. We all help ourselves to breakfast in the kitchen. There is plenty of fun as well as hard work and I can thoroughly recommend an Arvon Course to anyone who is keen to improve his or her writing. Contact the appropriate centre for details.

Similar courses are offered by the Welsh Taliesin Trust at

Ty Newydd Writers Centre, Llanystumdwy, Criccieth, Gwynedd. LL52 0LW; email tynewydd@dial.pipex.com

Distance learning

The Open College of the Arts provides distance learning courses for those who prefer this method or are unable to travel to writing centres or writing groups. It offers a variety of courses including writing and the length of time for completion of the course is flexible. Full details are available from:

UK Residents: Open College of the Arts, Registration Department, Freepost SF10678, Barnsley S75 1BR. email: open.arts@ukonline.co.uk. website: www.oca-uk.com

Overseas: Open College of the Arts, Registration Department, Unit 1B, Redbrook Business Park, Wilthorpe Road, Barnsley, United Kingdom, S75 1JN.

Writers' conferences

There are several writers' conferences held annually in Britain for a weekend or a whole week and there are many worldwide. Here are some of the most popular annual conferences:

The Writers' Summer School, Swanwick, Derbyshire. The Secretary, Writers' Summer School, 10 Stag Road, Lake Sandown, Isle of Wight PO36 8PE. email: jean.sutton@lineone.net website : www.wss.org.uk

The Southern Writers' Conference, The Earnley Concourse, Chichester, Sussex (a weekend in June). Details from Lucia White, Stable House, Home Farm, Coldharbour Lane, Dorking, Surrey RH4 8JG.

Annual Writers' Conference at King Alfred's College, Winchester, Hampshire. Contact Mrs Barbara Large MBE FRSA, Conference Director, Chinook, Southdown Road, Shawford, Hampshire SO21 2BY.
email: WriterConf@aol.com Telephone: +44(0)1962 712307
www.gmp.co.uk/writers/conference/

Always enclose a stamped self-addressed envelope when requesting information.

Writing magazines

There are two excellent magazines for aspiring writers, available by subscription: the bi-monthly *Writers' Forum*, PO Box 3229, Bournemouth, Dorset BH1 1ZS. email writintl@globalnet.co.uk and the monthly subscription magazine *Writers' News* – published by Yorkshire Post Newspapers Ltd, PO Box 168, Wellington Street, Leeds LS1 IRF. email: Christine.Sheppard@ypn.co.uk

The bi-monthly *Writing* magazine is available in major bookshops as well as to subscribers of *Writers' News*. Readers in the USA will find valuable information in *The Writer's Handbook 2002* edited by Elfrieda Abbe, published by The Writer Inc., 120 Boylston Street, Boston MA 12116, which also publishes a monthly magazine *The Writer*. For further details visit www.writermag.com/

Online writing classes

WritingClasses.com
www.writingclasses.com/

The online division of the Gotham Writers' Workshop, New York. Classes are held in New York City or online. Courses usually run for 10 weeks, and each session lasts 3 hours. Courses cover a wide range of writing subjects at a variety of levels from beginner to master class. Online courses are also available. The website is superbly organized showing you how online classes work.

trAce Online Writing School
www.trace.ntu.ac.uk/
Online courses covering a wide range of subjects and also writers' workshops. An online writing community.

Worldwide writers' conferences and courses

Shaw guides
www.writing.shawguides.com/

Shaw's Directory has just under 2000 forthcoming writers' conferences on its list. Find the one you want and email for details. Countries include: US, Canada, Australia and the UK.

Search for writing conferences worldwide by genre including: autobiography/memoirs; children's fiction; horror; humour; journalism; mystery; non-fiction; play writing; poetry; romance; science fiction; screen writing; travel writing and young adult.

Search by month of the year, by country, genre.

The Complete Creative Writing Course
The Groucho Club, London.
www.creative-writing.pwp.blueyonder.co.uk/

Two ten-week fiction writing courses held on Saturday and Monday afternoons. They include discussion, exercises and criticism. Contact: The Complete Creative Writing Course, 82 Forest Road, London E8 3BH.

Australia

Education Network of Australia (EdNA) online Education
Network of Australia. www.edna.edu.au/

Australia's gateway to education and training resources and services. Enables you to search for Adult Community Education by location and subject.

South Australia: Adult Community Education Courses including creative writing. Go to www.tafe.sa.gov.au/; select *Adult Community Education*. A wide range of courses at many locations in South Australia on offer. Very similar philosophy to the UK Adult Education Service – Lifelong Learning.

Storyworks: Courses designed to develop creativity through the writing of personal memoirs and autobiographies. Courses are based in Sydney, Australia or online via email. Contact Bridget Brandon, Storyworks, PO Box 3035, Waverley, NSW 2024, Australia. email: bridgetbrandon@storyworks.com.au

Canada

Simon Fraser University: Writing and Publishing Program
www.sfu.ca/

Wide range of courses ranging from a full certificate in creative writing to individual courses on specific topics. Contact: Simon Fraser University at Harbour Centre, 515 West Hastings Street, Vancouver, B.C. Canada V6B 5K3.

The Humber School for Writers
www.admin.humberc.on.ca/

Summer workshop in July (accommodation available). Contact: The Humber School for Writers, Humber College, 205 Humber College Blvd., Toronto, Ontario, Canada M9W 5L7.

Victoria School of Writing

Non-profit society offering a summer school, autumn and winter short courses, a spring literary information fair and postcard story contest, and year-round public readings. Contact: Victoria School of Writing Society, Box 8152, Victoria, BC, V8W 3R8. email: vicwrite@islandnet.com

Creative writing courses in New Zealand

New Zealand Ministry of Education
www.minedu.govt.nz/

Directory of New Zealand
www.directorynz.co.nz

Enter "creative writing" to access well over 1000 references to creative writing including courses at every level.

Creative Writing at the Victoria University of Wellington, New Zealand: International Institute of Modern Letters.
www.vuw.ac.nz/modernletters/

Post-graduate and undergraduate courses. MA in creative writing, Victoria University of Wellington, P.O. Box 600, Wellington, New Zealand.
email: modernletters@vuw.ac.nz

Fiona Kidman Creative Writing School
www.kidmancreative.co.nz/

Administered by the Whitireia Community Polytechnic. It offers writers' workshops and summer schools. Contact: NZ Payroll House, 126 Lambton Quay, Wellington, New Zealand
email: wellington@whitireia.ac.nz

Continuing Education at the University of Auckland
  www.cce.auckland.ac.nz/

Go to *Community Courses* for a range of writing courses
including getting started to travel writing and the novel. Writing
weeks in the summer and autumn workshops. Contact:
Continuing Education, Te Ara Pukenga, The University of
Auckland, 22 Princes Street, Auckland, New Zealand.

USA

Associated Writing Programs
  www.awpwriter.org/

Comprehensive listing of AWP Higher Education courses from
Alaska to Wyoming with full contact details, most with web
addresses. Started in 1967 the Association now comprises 20,000
individual writers, teachers, and students and 320 college and
university creative writing programmes in the United States,
Canada, and the United Kingdom.

Indiana University Writers' Conference, Bloomington, Indiana.
  http://php.indiana.edu/~iuwc/

Established in 1940, participants in the week-long conference
held in June join faculty-led workshops in fiction and poetry, take
classes on various aspects of writing, engage in one-on-one
consultation with faculty members, and attend a variety of
readings and social events. Accommodation is available. Contact:
Amy Locklin, Director, Indiana University Writers' Conference,
464 Ballantine Hall, Bloomington, Indiana 47405. email:
alocklin@indiana.edu

Alternatively try: Leslie Leisure, Assistant Director at:

email: lleasure@indiana.edu

Haystack Writing Program
  www.haystack.pdx.edu/writing/

Established in 1968, the programme runs from the first week in
June through to the first week in August. Week-long and weekend
courses are available, covering a wide range of topics. Contact:
Elizabeth Snyder, Haystack Writing Program, Portland State
University, School of Extend Studies, PO Box 1491, Portland,
Oregon 97207-1491. email: snydere@ses.pdx.edu

Continuing Studies at the University of Wisconsin-Madison
  www.dcs.wisc.edu/

This programme offers creative fiction and non-fiction writing. You register for the programme or workshop that interests you and attend without having to join a full university course. Contact: Continuing Studies, 905 University Avenue, Madison, WI 53715, 608-262-1156. email info@dcs.wisc.edu

21

the writer and technology

In this chapter you will learn:
- the benefits and limitations of the computer for the writer
- the communication benefits of the internet for the writer.

If you started writing from scratch – with just a pencil, an A4 pad and a head full of ideas – you already know how economical a hobby writing can be! But the next stage, that is, getting your work into good enough shape to send to an editor, will be a little more costly.

You could minimize the cost by buying a used typewriter or 'dedicated' word processor. This might see you through in the short-term. In the longer term, if you plan to take your writing further, you'll find a computer will help enormously and in many more ways than just producing a professional looking manuscript. As we will see, it needn't cost the earth.

In this chapter we will look at some of the things a computer can (and can't) do to help your writing and in the next we'll see what resources would also become available to you if you connected it to the internet.

If you are new to computers ...

The plain fact is that a writer needs only a basic computer with a good word processing program, internet access and a decent printer.

The fastest, biggest, most expensive computers are for those who want to do other things such as record and edit moving pictures, capture live TV, store and edit large quantities of hi fi quality music and play high speed games in 3D. The good thing about this trend towards bigger, 'better', faster computers is that it means there is a thriving second-hand market and you might consider this as an option providing you can find an established local dealer with a good reputation. Your writers' circle may be able to advise you here, passing on their good (and bad) experiences.

From the computer's point of view, the things a writer wants it to do are *easy*! If there's one thing even the most basic computer can handle with ease it's text and, these days, photographs are probably the next easiest.

All a writer needs from a computer is the ability to process and store text and the means to print it out onto paper. Being able to gather information from the internet is optional but as you have probably noticed throughout this book the Web can provide a wealth of information. Add to that the ability to communicate via email and instantly send your synopsis and opening chapter anywhere in the world (if requested to do so) and the internet is too attractive to miss.

Not so very long ago getting 'into' computers meant first learning all about them and becoming a 'computer buff' along the way. But that certainly isn't true now. The great thing today is that you don't have to learn what you don't need to know – just as you can drive a car around the world without even knowing how to undo the bonnet – provided nothing goes wrong and you've chosen the car wisely. There is nothing to fear!

What technology can do to help the writer

When you buy a computer make sure there is a word processing program included (the favourites are Microsoft *Word*, Lotus *Word Pro*, Corel *WordPerfect*). They all have step-by-step help guides available on screen and these are very user friendly. If you feel you would like a bit of extra help then there are computer courses for beginners of all ages which will help to get you started using the computer and/or the internet.

The word processing program will offer a wide range of editing facilities including the following main points:

1 It takes the chore out of typing, enabling you to produce a fully corrected manuscript before committing it to paper.
2 Your documents can have uniform formatting – margins, line length, lines per page, etc.
3 It will number the pages automatically, regardless of how many deletions and insertions you may make, updating them as you go.
4 It can place the title and your name on every page either top or bottom. Type it in once and that's it.
5 It will provide you with a word count for the whole document or for a chosen section.
6 You can *copy* a whole section and place it in another part of the document – or in another file entirely.
7 You can *move* a whole section and place it in another part of the document – or in another file entirely.
8 You can delete as much or as little as you wish.
9 You can make text bold or italicize sections of text or single words or underline words and titles.

10 You can keep different versions of your work as it develops. Some word processor programs allow you to keep track of different versions on screen showing additions and deletions.

11 You can produce a bulleted list to make your points clearer.

12 You can vary the size of the display on the screen to make reading more comfortable.

Think of the computer as a giant filing cabinet. The drawers of the cabinet are the major 'directories' which you can create – such as, say, writing, finance, photographs and household matters. Within each of the directories you might arrange your files under sub-headings or sub-directories, for example, writing might be divided into short stories, novels, poetry, ideas, work in progress, market information and so on. So, when you create a new file on your computer you place it in the appropriate section and can then find it easily later.

If you're wondering just how big that 'giant' filing cabinet is and how much it can store, well, the humble floppy disk can comfortably store a 100,000 word novel. The reason the floppy disk is 'humble' is that it can't store very much information compared to other storage mediums. It would be easy to get into reams of statistics but today's minimum size hard disk drive can store six gigabytes of data. This is the main storage medium inside the computer and at that size is capable of storing more than 4,000 floppy disks worth of information.

Added to this, the newest machines perform the tasks which are set them with incredible speed. But how fast does a writer need the machine to be? A three-year-old machine, not exactly 'top of the range', can load the 12 chapters of a 75,000 novel in less than 15 seconds! So, speed is not an issue.

A couple of clicks of the mouse switches the display from, say, Chapter 1 to Chapter 12. Any of the chapters is available on screen individually for editing. More than one chapter can be displayed on the screen at a time to compare them or simply to check details, that is, Chapter 3 in the top half of the screen and Chapter 8 in the bottom half.

Apart from storage and editing facilities, the computer can provide you with quick on-screen reference whilst working. Encyclopaedias, thesauri, dictionaries of words, quotations and phrases are all affordable and some highly respected ones are even given away free with computer magazines on CD-ROMs for home use. These reference works contain just as much, if not more, than the printed version but have the immense advantage over the book in that they are *searchable*. This means you can enter a key word and the search engine will quickly go through the entire text to find all references to that word and offer links to those references. Having such a powerful tool at your fingertips means that you can step out of the piece you are writing to check a word, find an alternative, check a reference, fact or date in the encyclopaedia and all without leaving your seat!

What technology can't do to help the writer

It can't think for you and it can't write the next scene or the next sentence. We have already seen in Chapter 12, Revision with Style that the spelling and grammar checkers are helpful but have limitations. So is this the end for pen and paper? Not quite. Many writers combine the advantages of both by doing the earlier drafts of their work on a good old-fashioned pad, getting it roughly correct in creative terms before moving to the computer to type it up, making more changes along the way. The next draft can then be printed out ready for further corrections.

If you are just starting out a computer is not absolutely necessary – not yet. You can work around the lack of a computer and produce professional looking manuscripts using a typewriter or dedicated word processor but, as I hope the above shows, you can do so much more with a computer. It is becoming a distinct disadvantage not to have an email address. So let's move on to the other part of this chapter – the basics of the internet.

The internet

Not all computers can access the internet. To do that it must be equipped with a gadget called a modem. This can be either internal or external. If it's already fitted internally all you will see is a wire coming from the back of the computer which will have a phone connector on the end of it. You plug this into your phone socket. Unless you have two separate phone lines you will not be able to make or receive phone calls whilst you are actually 'on line', that is, actively connected to the internet.

It is the Internet Service Provider (ISP) who enables you to get on line such as AOL or Freeserve or Compuserve.

The internet allows you to visit or view the web pages of your choice but you need to know the address and that's where all the www stuff comes in, that is, the BBC's web address is www.bbc.co.uk. This will take you to the BBC's home page. As you can imagine there are many many different departments and you can visit the one you want by following the *links*. As you move the mouse the on-screen pointer will move correspondingly but will change shape when it comes to certain words or links, for example, Arts. If Arts is the department you want then you click the left button of the mouse whilst the on-screen pointer is over the word Arts and the screen will change as you are taken to the Arts web page. There you will find another range of choices, and you follow these 'links' until you come to the section you want, for example, The Writers' Room.

Emails

Along with the internet comes the ability to send and receive emails. Here the international aspect of the internet will be really brought home to you, literally, when you send an email to New York and get a reply within minutes. You can send text or pictures 'attached' to the email, for example, a selected file from your computer, such as a short story or an article.

Message boards and newsgroups

You can contribute to 'message boards' in the subject area or areas of your choice. This means that you can post a message and over a period of time other people respond and a 'discussion' builds up. For example, there's a writers' message board at the BBC website as part of The Writers' Room (www.bbc.co.uk/writersroom). Here, once you have registered with the site, you can ask a writing question and then check back later to see if anyone has answered. Newsgroups are similar and are used mainly to share information and news on a given topic.

Chat rooms

You can also join 'chat rooms' for more immediate online discussion where what you type in will be seen by others virtually without delay. There are designated topic areas and it is advisable to sit back at first and gauge the flow of the discussion before making a contribution. This can be quite time consuming. Occasionally a television programme will continue a discussion over onto the web. This allows viewers to ask a question or join in the discussion via their computers. Transcripts of these sessions appear on the website for later reference. There is an archive of interviews/discussions with writers at the Writers' Room page at the BBC site.

Message boards, newsgroups and chat rooms are useful tools for a writer if used properly and sparingly. There is a real danger that this activity could take up more of your writing time than you originally intended. Don't let it. Chapter 22, Research and the Internet explores the internet further and includes references and resources. *The Internet: A Writer's Guide*, by Jane Dorner (A & C Black), is an excellent book which will guide you through the entire process of getting connected and using the internet. It's an invaluable guide for writers.

Further reading

Teach Yourself The Internet for Writers, by John Ralph (Hodder & Stoughton).

22

research and the internet

In this chapter you will learn:
- how the computer and the internet can help your research
- useful web addresses providing the latest on markets and competitions
- useful web addresses providing reference support for all subjects.

In this chapter we will look at how the internet can help you take your first steps in researching a particular subject followed by a list of some of the writers' resources available on the internet (see below, References and resources). At the end of the chapter there's also a list of recommended reference books.

As an example, let's take a popular type of feature – the researched article commemorating an important event or birthday. To have a chance with this sort of article you need to look well ahead. Let's take the year 2006 and see what anniversaries will fall in that year.

The best place to start is usually the encyclopaedia. In this case I used Microsoft's *Encarta, Encyclopaedia Deluxe 2001* – offline, that is, without connecting to the internet. This highly regarded encyclopaedia comes on CD-ROMs for your computer. I asked it to find references to the year 1906 which it did almost instantly. As you can imagine, quite a long list resulted and this needed filtering but here are a few examples. The year 2006 will see the centenary of the birth of former poet laureate Sir John Betjeman, former Labour leader Hugh Gaitskell, composer Elisabeth Agnes Lutyens, film directors John Huston, Anthony Mann and Sir Carol Reed, screenwriter and director Billy Wilder and financier John D. Rockefeller. It will also be the centenary anniversary of the 'birth' of the Kellog Company, the London Ritz, and the word 'genetics'. 1906 also saw the publication of the first 'instalment' of John Glasworthy's *The Forsyte Saga* ('*A Man of Property*') and it was the year of the San Francisco Earthquake.

The internet as a research tool

Now let's choose one of those topics – Sir John Betjeman – and research it in greater depth using the internet.

Using a search engine

There are many search engines – Google, Alta Vista, Yahoo, Ask Jeeves, Lycos. They all have their different strengths and advantages. Let's use Google. Once online, the first thing to do is to type Google's address into the address bar of the browser (usually at the top of the screen) – www.google.com

Once the site has been reached and appears on the screen, typing "John Betjeman" – enclosed in inverted commas – into the search box results in a list (covering several screens) of 6240 web references found in 0.18 seconds! Top of the list is John Betjeman's official website which offers: examples of his work, photographs, bibliography, a biography, a shop and links to other websites.

So gathering facts about Betjeman is fairly easy. It's a bit like walking into a giant library to find that the helpful librarian had gathered together all of the references to your subject opened at the relevant page ready for your inspection.

If you eventually decided to use quotes from his work this website would be a good place to start in gaining permission to do so. Here you will find details of the Betjeman Society and they would be able to put you on the right track.

Of course, not all the 6240 web references are worth following through but the brief descriptions provided by the search engine will give enough information to whet your appetite – or not. You can start to build up a fact file on Sir John's life and works and along the way you may find the *angle* for the article you will eventually write.

As covered in Chapter 3, How to Write an Article, the angle is the particular, unusual slant you will give a topic, for example, Sir John was a fervent preservationist with a passionate interest in the English countryside and architecture. So perhaps somewhere in there is the angle – Sir John Betjeman died in 1984, what would he think of modern developments?

You may now find your researches taking you in new directions. As with any topic the angle will probably occur to you as you gather interesting material and begin to look for the article within it.

Two final thoughts on using the internet as a research tool. You still have to cross-check. Not all websites are factually reliable. The quality of the information on the internet is variable and has to be checked. The quality of your research will stem from the reliability of the sources you consult and they must be up to date and authoritative.

And finally, let Wendy Cope have the last word on research:

The Law of Copyright (after Kipling) by Wendy Cope

Now this is the Law of Copyright – good subject for Poetry Day.
If you keep it some poets may prosper, in a modest and limited way.

And some of the people who break it have little idea the wrong
They do to the indigent author who dreamed up the poem or song

That they put into print without asking, or perform in a theatre or hall
With an audience paying good money, while the writer gets nothing at all,

Or offer the world on their web-sites, assuming that poems are free.
They are shocked when you mention permission, aghast if there's talk of a fee.

This is the law: the creator has rights that you can't overlook.
It isn't OK to make copies – you have to fork out for the book.

It isn't OK to use poems on posters or cards or in shows
Unless you have asked for permission. You may have to pay through the nose

But not necessarily. Try it. If you're a good cause, or you're poor,
And unlikely to make any profit, the cost of obeying the law

May be negligible, may be nothing. It's one thing to ask for a gift
And another to take without asking, and we call that other thing theft.

And poets they need to eat supper, and poets they need to wear shoes
And you'll seldom encounter a poet enjoying a luxury cruise,

So remember the Law of Copyright, and make sure you do as you ought,
And if you read this and ignore it, I bloody well hope you get caught.

Reprinted by permission of PFD on behalf of Wendy Cope

The internet as a source of market information

Australia

www.nla.gov.au/oz/litsites

The National Library of Australia website provides an extensive resource devoted to Australian arts and literature including a section on awards and contests plus links to all the major Australian literary sites.

UK

See entry for Jacqui Bennett's Writing Bureau below under Markets, competitions and awards.

US and Canada:

www.fictionhouse.com

Fiction House, The Creative Writers' Resource provides a huge amount of information including markets and contests

New Zealand

www.nzweb.co.nz

Enter Writers Markets and this will give you access to a full array of writers' resources.

As a communication tool

As you have seen above, email enables you not only to send messages and attach files and pictures but also to keep up to date with news and competitions. There are many free newsletters which you can subscribe to which will arrive in your mail box automatically and keep you well informed.

As a reference library

Below you will find just a few suggestions of useful websites you might like to try. There are many many more.

References and resources

BBC websites

BBC Arts

www.bbc.co.uk/arts/books/

News and interviews, author profiles – a good 'gateway' site to all the other writing strands on the BBC site including The Writers' Room which is recommended.

BBC Radio 4

www.bbc.co.uk/radio4

Listen to programmes online at a time to suit you. Lots of news, views and message boards.

BBC World Service

Excellent How to Write ... page includes How to Write: a Novel, Memoir, Screenplay, Radio Drama, plus tips from Robert McKee and Martin Amis.

Online dictionaries

AskOxford

www.askoxford.com

Better writing, word games, classic errors and helpful hints.

Cambridge Dictionaries

www.dictionary.cambridge.org/

Cambridge Dictionaries Online is an excellent website and very easy to use. It provides UK definitions as well as American and Australian spellings.

Merriam-Webster Online

www.m-w.com/

US site. Collegiate dictionary, collegiate thesaurus, word games, word of the day.

World Wide Words

www.quinion.com/words

Investigating International English from a British viewpoint. Huge site, interesting and searchable.

Xrefer

www.xrefer.com/

Xrefer is a huge reference site. Type in a word and see examples of it in use, quoted from many different dictionaries and encyclopaedias. Refine your search by searching in one of the following: art, British history, business and law, dictionaries, encyclopaedia, English literature, health, language and usage, music, philosophy, place names, quotations, science, technology, thesaurus.

Markets, competitions and awards

Jacqui Bennett Writers Bureau

www.jbwb.co.uk/

Excellent site offering comprehensive market information in all areas of writing plus competition news, home study courses and mini courses for writers worldwide. Associated with the Home Study division of *Writer's News*.

Midland Exposure Literary Agency

www.midlandexposure.co.uk/

Good site with a strong links section. Especially interesting for new magazine writers seeking a breakthrough. Regular market-based competitions in May and November each year.

Poets and writers

www.pw.org/mag/

Online version of the informative US magazine which includes news and a comprehensive list of competitions and conferences.

The Book Trust

www.booktrust.org.uk

Prizes, projects, information and advice includes details of the Fidler Award for unpublished children's writers.

The Scottish Book Trust

www.scottishbooktrust.com/

Information on Scottish Book Trust plus details of the highly respected Fidler Award for a first novel for children aged 8–12 years.

Names

BabyCentre

www.babycenter.com/babyname

US site. Discover the meaning and origin of names from many ethnic cultures. Charts for the most popular names since the 1880s.

Eponym

www.eponym.org

Another site providing lists of names arranged in popularity order, as well as a strong list of other name sites.

Newspapers and magazines

Guardian Unlimited
www.guardian.co.uk/Books/
Reviews, interviews, first chapters. Excellent site. Includes a link to the *Observer* newspaper.

The Paper Boy
www.thepaperboy.co.uk/
Links to all the major UK newspapers, online versions go to www.thepaperboy.com which puts the world's newspapers at your fingertips. A fabulous resource.

The Telegraph
www.telegraph.co.uk
Keep up to date with book reviews, etc., plus articles and interviews with this online version of the *Daily Telegraph*.

Organizations

PEN
www.pen.org.uk/public
World association of writers, looking after writers' interests since 1921. It's first president was John Galsworthy.

The Society of Authors
www.societyofauthors.org
Full details of the benefits of joining and how to go about it.

The Writers Guild of Great Britain
www.writersguild.org.uk/
The TUC union for all professional writers.

Poetry

Bibliomania
www.bibliomania.com
Many free classic texts including Blake, Shelley, Keats and Chaucer.

The Peter Finch Archive
www.peterfinch.co.uk/sitemap.htm
Includes poetry by Peter Finch – traditional, experimental and Haiku – plus a very useful 'Writer's Advice' page.

The National Library For Poetry

www.poetrylibrary.org.uk

Here's a quote from the website: 'The most comprehensive and accessible collection of post–1910 poetry in Britain: It's a free public library open to all UK residents that can be used like any public library and where everyone is warmly welcomed; to join bring proof of name and address.' Excellent project.

The Poetry Kit

www.poetrykit.org/

International poetry site. Events page lists poetry events in US, Australia, Canada, New Zealand and the UK. Look up interviews, articles and poetry, magazines worldwide, courses, competitions and links to other sites.

The Poetry Society

www.poetrysociety.org.uk/

Details of the National Poetry Competition, poetry events, for example, National Poetry Day, online editions of the Poetry Review with selected articles available. Excellent site.

Word Circuits

www.wordcircuits.com

Experimental poetry which uses the internet in an interesting way, showcasing new work and making you think afresh about words – and poetry.

Quotations

Bartleby

www.bartleby.com

More than just quotations. A huge American site, this literary resource is particularly strong on language and quotations.

Quotation Reference

www.quotationreference.com/

Search for a quotation by author or subject.

Research

Ask a Librarian

www.ask-a-librarian.org.uk

Brings the resources of the UK library service to your desktop. Will also answer questions from overseas. Post a question and the librarian will email you the answer or point you in the right direction.

Canada: Answerline

www.tpl.toronto.on.ca/

Ask a question and get an email reply within 24 hours.

USA: Allexperts.com

www.allexperts.com/

Select your subject, select an expert in that subject and ask your question. Huge topic range. Free service.

Ingenta

www.ingenta.com/

Provides access to over 12,000,000 articles. You can search to find the right one then pay-to-view.

National Statistics

www.statistics.gov.uk/

The official UK statistics site. You can view and download a wealth of social and economic data – free. A fully searchable, easy to use site.

Search engines

Ask Jeeves

www.ask.co.uk

Enables you to ask a question in plain English. It attempts to break down the key words you have used to offer a variety of routes to find out the answer.

Google

www.google.co.uk

www.google.com (US site)

Not only fast and simple to use but also includes a directory which will lead you to specific topic areas. For *Writing* go to *Directory, Arts, Writers' Resources* to put yourself in touch with over 3000 writing orientated websites.

Style and grammar

Cliché Finder

www.westegg.com/cliche/

An index of 3300 clichés, you can add to the list, search for a cliché including a specified word, for example, 'cat' or see a list of ten random clichés. Great fun.

Guardian Unlimited

www.guardian.co.uk/styleguide

You can download this very useful guide which will help you in the preparation of your final draft, for example, should we say 'an' hotel or 'a' hotel? The style guide says 'a' hotel.

Oxford Dictionaries

www.askoxford.com/betterwriting/
Includes better writing, classic errors, helpful hints, word games, word of the day.

Theatre

The Internet Theatre Bookshop

www.stageplays.com/
Comprehensive catalogue of stage plays.

Writing tips, articles, resources

Author.co.uk

www.author.co.uk/
UK site for writers and publishers includes news and articles and a comprehensive writers' advice section plus details of self publishing.

Writing exercises

Michelle Richmond's website: www.michellerichmond.com/exercise is a collection of exercises compiled during US writer Michelle Richmond's six years as Creative Writing Tutor at the Gotham Writers' Workshop in New York City, The Writing Salon in San Francisco, the University of Miami, and the California College of Arts and Crafts.

Today's exercise? Write about something you hope you never have to do.

Writing World

www.writing-world.com/
A massive site. A good tip is when you reach the *home page* go to the Site Index option at the top of the page and click on it. You will find a huge array of articles on writing classified by subject. Also on this site: writing competitions in the US, Canada and the UK, arranged ahead by closing dates, as well as advanced writing tips and online writing classes.

Reference books

There are three books every writer should have on his desk: a good dictionary, *Roget's Thesaurus of English Words and Phrases* and the current edition of *The Writers' and Artists' Yearbook* or *The Writer's Handbook* (in America *The Writer's Market* or *The Novel & Short Story Writer's Market*).

Dictionaries

For quick reference *Collins Concise Dictionary* or *The Penguin English Dictionary* are ideal, but you should really have a more extensive dictionary as well.

The following are recommended: *The Shorter Oxford English Dictionary; Collins English Dictionary; The Chambers Dictionary; Merriam-Webster's New Collegiate; The Oxford Modern English Dictionary.*

The following books are also very useful and may be consulted in most public reference libraries:

Fowler's Modern English Usage (OUP);
Strunk and White's Elements of Style (Allyn and Bacon);
Teach Yourself Correct English (Hodder and Stoughton);
Brewer's Dictionary of Phrase and Fable (Cassell);
Encyclopaedia Britannica (Encyclopaedia Britannica Inc.);
Oxford Dictionary of Quotations (OUP);
Oxford Desk Dictionary of People and Places, (OUP);
The Oxford Dictionary for Writers and Editors (OUP).

Willings Press Guide is a comprehensive guide to newspapers, magazines, business and specialist publications in the UK. Useful information can also be found in the Overseas Volume of *Willings Press Guide* (Media Information) available in most reference libraries. For details of more reference books see the Bibliography at the end of this book.

For your computer

Available on CD-ROM:

The Encarta Encyclopedia Deluxe (Microsoft)

The Encarta World Dictionary (Microsoft)

The New Shorter Oxford English Dictionary (OUP)

Exercise 40

'Write about something you hope you never have to do.'

Explore this topic either from a personal, non-fiction perspective or from the point of view of one of your characters. Maximum 1000 words.

23

editors, publishers and literary agents

In this chapter you will learn:

- the role of the editor
- the role of the publisher
- the role of the literary agent.

Editors

The aspiring writer, sending out manuscripts and waiting in trepidation for the postman to bring them back, is sometimes inclined to develop a sort of persecution mania after a long succession of rejections. One certainly feels helpless; the editorial staff decides what is to be published, and the rejected author has no right to query or complain.

On the other hand, one has only to put oneself in the editor's place to understand that many writers are bound to be disappointed. Some magazines receive hundreds of unsolicited manuscripts a week, and out of that number only a small proportion is up to publication standard. Staff writers and regular contributors provide a good deal of the material and there is also a reserve of accepted freelance work to draw upon.

This does not mean to say that contributions from unknown writers are not of great importance; editors are constantly on the lookout for promising newcomers, and every manuscript is carefully considered. A practised eye, however, can see from the first page – sometimes from the first sentence – whether or not a short story or an article is well written. There are a great many unpublished manuscripts around; many beginners have no idea how much technical skill and hard work are needed in order to produce a saleable piece of work.

Editors have a very difficult and exhausting job. Most of them understand the problems and the heartaches of the novice and do all they can to encourage new talent and ease the disappointment of those who lack the necessary skills. It is quite impossible, however, in the vast majority of cases for them to state the reasons for refusal. As I have said before, there simply isn't time.

When you find a returned manuscript lying on the mat – a bulky envelope instead of the hoped-for thin one – bear in mind that it has not *necessarily* been rejected because it is not good enough. The editor may recently have accepted an article or story on a similar theme, your piece may in some way be in conflict with editorial policy or there could be a personal reason why that particular editor does not find it acceptable.

You must be confident, hard-working and resilient to succeed in the tough competitive world of magazine publishing. If you can picture yourself in an editorial chair, faced every morning with a mountain of manuscripts, many of them the wrong length, ungrammatical, badly typed with the pages unnumbered and copious alterations scribbled illegibly in the margins, you will understand the difficulties.

Be patient. Writers and editors need each other. The writer, while bearing in mind that he must supply outstanding material, should never lose sight of the fact that the editor could not produce a single copy of a magazine without his authors.

Publishers

Publishers, like editors, come in for occasional abuse from writers. I think it has something to do with power. Nobody likes to feel that he is a helpless pawn in any game and the novice can hardly escape that feeling when he sends the typescript of his first book to a publisher. We are all inclined to resist authority (especially the writer, who is often a strong individualist and a bit of a rebel by nature) and we hate to be in a position of such total subservience. ('Who does he think he is, not accepting my book!')

The publisher, like the editor, is continually faced with an avalanche of amateur typescripts, any one of which might be a work of genius but most of which are not. If every writer would send a preliminary letter before dispatching a parcel there would be far fewer cases of stress and distress among both publishers and authors.

You know all about the writer's problems; now let's have a look at the problems of the publisher. It costs many thousands of pounds to publish and distribute a book and so he must obviously feel confident of making reasonable sales before he accepts a manuscript. It's up to you, as the writer, to study your craft and work diligently to produce a book which is so original, so readable and so professionally organized that the publisher you choose will see it as an attractive business proposition as well as a work of art.

If your manuscript is refused, with no reason given except that their 'lists are full', don't be discouraged. Many successful books were sent to more than a dozen publishers before they were accepted, including *Room at the Top*, *Catch 22* and *Watership Down*. My own *Craft of Novel-Writing* went to 26 and was then published simultaneously in hardback and paperback. It is still in print today. Provided you are confident that the book is as good as you can make it, keep on trying and at last you may receive the letter you dream of.

Let's assume that you have in fact received that letter. A publisher likes your book and is prepared to offer you a contract. He will probably suggest a meeting at this stage so that you can get to know one another over lunch and discuss the book. If you are a new writer he will want to hear about your future plans, so think them out before you see him.

The next thing is for him to draw up a contract which will eventually be signed by both of you. (If you employ a literary agent he will have his own form of contract.) The contract is a legal document setting out the points which must be agreed before the book can be published, notably the percentage of the selling price which you will receive. You should never sell the copyright of your book for a lump sum; few publishers would expect it. You will probably be offered from ten to 15 per cent on the hardback edition, depending on the number of copies sold (perhaps ten per cent for the first 2500, 12 for the next 2500 and 15 thereafter). These percentages will vary according to the publisher, the type of book and your professional standing.

Your book will probably take up to a year to appear in print, but six months or so after the delivery of your final manuscript, the proofs will arrive for correction. You are allowed about two weeks to check them carefully for printing errors. This is *not* the time to revise your book! Your typescript must be as near perfect as you can make it before it goes to the printers. Proof corrections are expensive and there will be a clause in your contract committing you to pay for any corrections of your own above a certain amount. (Printers' mistakes, of course, are not your responsibility except for spotting them!) Proof correcting should hold no fears for you; the *Writers' and Artists' Yearbook* gives clear instructions on the use of the correct symbols.

Vanity publishing

Never pay to have a book (except perhaps of poetry) published; if your manuscript is worthy of publication, sooner or later it will be accepted and royalties paid in the normal way. An unscrupulous 'vanity' publisher will praise your book to the skies and make impossible promises in order to persuade you to part with your money. He will also try to convince you that it is now the norm for authors to contribute towards the cost of publication. It isn't.

Finally, remember that the author's relationship with his publisher is a very delicate one. We all long for the ideal publisher who will appreciate the hard work we do, understand our problems, produce our books in a beautiful format with a superb jacket, advertise widely, provide regular sales figures, pay up on time – and accept our next book without a quibble.

The publisher, I think, must dream of the following virtues in his authors: neatness and accuracy, punctual delivery of manuscripts and corrected proofs, a minimum of letters and phone calls, a good humoured professional approach and, last but not least, a regular output of highly marketable books!

If you have a book published you could receive payment under a scheme known as Public Lending Right (PLR) on condition that you have registered with their office. The fee is calculated on the number of times your book is borrowed from public libraries and is provided by the Government. Write for details to Public Lending Right, Richard House, Sorbonne Close, Stockton-on-Tees TS17 6DA (www.plr.uk.com).

Literary agents

If you were to eavesdrop on two successful authors there's every chance that they would be talking about their agents. And it would probably be quite a heated discussion:

> 'My agent is hopeless. He takes his ten per cent and does absolutely nothing for me. He never answers my letters and now that I want to leave him I can't get my manuscripts back.'

> 'Really? Oh, I'm terribly lucky. Mine couldn't be more helpful. She's earned me thousands over the years...'

So how do you go about finding a reliable agent?

The wisest approach is to go by personal recommendation, but if you are out of touch with professional writers you should refer to the *Writers' and Artists' Yearbook* or *The Writer's Handbook*.

Many authors manage quite well without an agent but if you are a dreamy kind of person with little or no business experience, I think you would be well advised to look for one. (I'm only talking about books; few agents are interested in articles, short stories or plays by beginners.)

Let's consider the advantages of employing an agent:

- He knows the most suitable publishers for your particular manuscript and will send it out (many times, if need be) at no extra cost. You don't pay him a penny until he has found you a publisher and then he will deduct the usual ten per cent plus VAT from your royalties. Avoid any agent who charges a reading fee.

- He will draw up a fair contract, doing 'battle' with your publisher, if necessary, to secure better terms.
- He will explore the possibilities of paperback rights, serial rights, radio and television rights, and so on. Having contacts in many parts of the world, he is in an ideal position to negotiate foreign rights.
- He will look after your financial interests, making sure that you receive payment on time.
- He will advise you on all matters connected with your work, although he cannot be expected to do more than minor editing.
- Manuscripts received from a reputable agent are often put at the top of the pile on a publisher's desk. All manuscripts are given careful consideration in due course, but if you employ an agent you might well receive priority treatment.
- Knowing your abilities, he might obtain a commission for you to write a book. Mine did.

It is not always easy for a new writer to find an agent who is prepared to take him on; naturally, your manuscript must appeal to him as a marketable commodity. Choose an agent who specializes in your type of work (see one of the 'Yearbooks') and send a preliminary letter describing your book very briefly and asking if he would be willing to consider it. If you receive a favourable reply, send him your manuscript or opening chapters – whichever he has requested – making sure that it has a good professional appearance and enclosing return postage.

If he is not prepared to take you on, he may or may not tell you why your book falls short of his requirements. If he does you should take careful note of his comments and consider revising your work accordingly. Don't spoil your chances of success for the want of a little humility. I've seen it happen too often.

If you are successful in finding an agent, don't keep badgering him about the fate of your manuscript. Leave him to send it out as he thinks fit; he will let you know at once if he has good news for you. He will expect to handle all your subsequent work and this is as it should be. You can look forward to many years of friendly cooperation with a business representative who has your interests very much at heart. After all, his livelihood depends on the success of his authors.

24

the professional approach

In this chapter you will learn:
- how to adopt a professional approach
- the basics of libel, income tax, copyright, moral rights and quotations
- how to cope with rejection slips.

It may be that you have no interest in the commercial aspect of writing and want to enjoy it as a private leisurely activity only, just for the love of it. This chapter is intended, as the heading implies, for those who have already seen their work in print or hope to do so one day.

When you are a beginner you are inclined to worry about matters which cease to trouble you when you become established. If you are still a novice, a few words of advice at this stage might help you to avoid those anxieties.

Try not to fret if a magazine spells your name wrongly, changes the title of your story, omits a vital paragraph or makes a printing error that gives the impression that you are illiterate! For years I used to be upset about such things, wasting nervous energy that might have been used creatively. At last, mainly through contact with professional writers, I learned to shrug off minor irritations, realizing that almost every writer has similar problems. Nevertheless, you must be firm in your complaint if you have a real grievance. An important aspect of the professional approach is to know when to take a stand and when to 'let it ride'.

Twelve points for new writers

1 Do your market research and keep it up to date.
2 Be sure that your typescripts are beyond reproach.
3 Don't be in a hurry to send out your work before you have revised it sufficiently.
4 Always enclose return postage when you submit a manuscript. If you send material overseas enclose sufficient International Reply Coupons to cover return postage by airmail or surface – one coupon is not usually enough even for a short article by air. These are obtainable from any Post Office.
5 Answer letters and emails promptly.
6 Keep your letters, phone calls and emails as brief as possible.
7 Don't mention personal problems if you can possibly avoid it.
8 Attend to the advice of editors and publishers with respect; it is usually valid.
9 Be accurate and up to date in all your facts.
10 Don't send out the same piece to more than one editor at the same time. (I should point out here that in exceptional circumstances – with topical material, for instance – a book may be sent to more than one publisher simultaneously. It must be stated that other publishers are also being approached but there is no need to say who they are.)

11 Don't forget that guidelines – even those given in this book – are no more than the name implies. They can be immensely helpful to the novice, but should not be followed too rigidly.
12 Don't be afraid to rewrite and keep trying.

When you begin to achieve some success you should consider joining the Society of Authors (84 Drayton Gardens, London SW10 9SB or www.societyofauthors.org) or the Writers' Guild of Great Britain (430 Edgware Road, London W2 1EH or www.writers.org.uk/guild). Writers in the US should contact the Writers' Guild of America, East, 555 West 57th Street, Suite 1230, New York, NY 10019. (www.wgaeast.org)

In my opinion it is incumbent upon every practising writer to belong, not only for the tremendous benefits (including the vetting of contracts) but also because we must band together to defend our rights. Authors, unless they are extremely successful, receive a pitifully low income compared with most other professions, and they are helpless to improve matters if they work alone.

As a would-be professional you will want to understand the rulings on income tax, copyright, libel and so on. Excellent articles on these matters can be found in our indispensable allies, the current *Writers' and Artists' Yearbook* and *The Writer's Handbook*. The laws are much too complex for me to explain in detail, but it might be helpful if I touch on some aspects as they concern the novice. You can extend your knowledge when you need to do so.

Libel

This is vaguely worrying for every published writer. We shall obviously write nothing which we *know* to be libellous but how can we be sure that some complete stranger, bearing the same name as the villain of one of our novels, will not sue us for defamation of character? We can't. We can only take reasonable precautions by checking the telephone book for the area in which the story is set, or even contacting the local Post Office to make sure that no one of that name is resident there. The well-known statement that 'the characters in this book are entirely fictitious and bear no resemblance to any actual person, alive or dead' carries no legal protection but it might deter a would-be troublemaker.

Income tax

This is a matter that will not concern you until you progress beyond the stage of writing as a hobby, but I strongly advise you to keep a careful record of your casual earnings and all your expenses for each financial year. The appropriate receipts should also be preserved. When you become successful, the losses incurred by previous expenses may be carried forward over a certain number of years and deducted from your taxable income. There are many points to consider but if you ask your tax inspector for advice you will usually find him helpful and cooperative in assessing your entitlements.

Copyright

As a general guide, the copyright of an author's writings – even a letter to a friend – belongs to him (or his estate) until 70 years after his death. After that time he may be quoted freely. (If he collaborated with another author, the copyright remains with the one who died last.) There is no copyright in ideas. If someone writes a story which is very similar to one of yours, you have no case for legal action unless it can be proved that the plot itself contains situations which have been deliberately stolen (i.e. plagiarized). It is quite possible for two people to hit on the same idea, even a very unusual one, and new writers are apt to get needlessly upset on this account. There is no copyright in titles.

There is also no copyright in facts, but it is illegal to copy the exact words of another author in stating them. That John Keats was born in October 1795 and died in Rome at the age of 25 are established facts and anyone may state them, but when a writer expresses a fact in his own individual way (even in an encyclopaedia) his actual words may not be reproduced without permission.

Moral rights

This is primarily the right of the author to be credited as the creator of the work whenever it is reproduced. There is also a secondary right of integrity which ensures that the author's work shall not be subjected to derogatory treatment or manipulation by the copyright holder (who may, in certain circumstances, be different from the author) in a manner which may harm the honour or reputation of the author.

In order for these rights to apply the moral rights of the author have to be asserted and this is done by means of a simple statement accompanying the work stating that the author wishes to assert his/her moral rights in the work. Moral rights are in addition to copyright.

Quotations

If you wish to quote from another author you must obtain written consent from his publisher, agent or whoever handles the quotation rights. Short extracts are usually allowed if they do not constitute 'a substantial part' of the work, which in practice generally means you can quote up to 50 words of prose without asking for consent. In the case of poetry, however, even a single line must be cleared for permission as it may form 'a substantial part' of the whole work. For reviews and serious works of literary criticism longer extracts are allowed, but the rules are complicated and in all forms of writing you should always inform your editor or publisher at the outset if you wish to use quotations, and be guided by him.

In *all* circumstances the quotation must be identified and proper acknowledgment made, so it is very important to note *full* details of all your sources as you go along. Make quite certain, too, that you have quoted accurately, including punctuation.

Permission to quote is seldom refused but a fee may be charged – sometimes quite a large one – and you should always wait for a reply before you commit yourself to a particular quotation. Payment is normally due on publication of the piece in question.

Complimentary copies

Non-writing friends and relatives will sometimes expect you to give them a copy of your latest book, duly inscribed. They do not realize that an author receives only six copies of each title free of charge from his publisher and that he will need to supply copies for his agent to send abroad in quest of foreign rights. You may, however, buy your own books from the publisher at trade price, although not to re-sell them.

The need for perseverance

I think it is usually a mistake to drag out old manuscripts and try to rehash them; it is better to forge ahead with something fresh. You are a more capable person now than you were a year ago – experience has seen to that: not only practice in writing but the people you have met, the problems you have faced, the stresses and successes, the imagining. Every experience, good and bad, can help us to become better writers, and that can be a comforting thought when we are going through a difficult patch in our lives.

One of the greatest enemies a novice has to face – and a professional, too, for that matter – is despondency. Our writing is so important to us that strong criticism from colleagues, rejection by editors or publishers, or simply a vague feeling of inadequacy, can be very depressing unless we dig in our heels and vow to persevere in spite of all setbacks. Many best-selling authors had to slog away for years before the breakthrough came; I know a popular television playwright who submitted more than 40 scripts before he had one accepted. Keep that in mind if you feel like giving up after two or three rejections!

My last piece of advice is one that I have sometimes ignored myself, with depressing results. *Be single-minded!* Finish what you are doing before you begin something else. If you have problems halfway through a novel (and who doesn't) don't break off and write short stories or start another book. Take a deep breath, pour yourself a stiff drink, say a prayer – or whatever suits you best (I like all three) – and make up your mind to get that novel right, even if it means going back to the beginning and starting again. Of course, there are occasions when you may genuinely lose interest in a project or realize that you are not yet ready to follow it through. This is rare, I think; the usual reasons for leaving something unfinished are laziness and fear of failure. Overcome these hazards and success will come much sooner.

Anne Sexton, the American poet and playwright, interviewed for the *Paris Review,* was asked what she thought a teacher could give a writer in a creative writing class. 'Courage, of course,' she replied. 'That's the most important ingredient.'

Later she was asked: 'What is the quality of feeling when you're writing?'

'Well, it's a beautiful feeling, even if it's hard work. When I'm writing I know I'm doing the thing I was born to do.'

I feel like that myself, and I hope it's going to be the same for you.

bibliography

Where books are still available for purchase, details of the latest edition are given – sources www.amazon.co.uk and www.bol.com

If a book is no longer easily available a search has been made on the internet to assess second-hand availability using the search engine of *Abebooks* – www.abebooks.com

Where a book has proved difficult to locate through usual retail outlets and the second-hand market the entry has been marked "Check with the library".

Walter Allen (ed.), *Writers on Writing,* Phoenix House, London, and E. P. Dutton, New York. (1948) Words about writing by some of the world's greatest writers. Both poetry and the novel are covered. Available second-hand via the internet.

Miriam Allott, *Novelists on the Novel,* Routledge and Kegan Paul, London and Boston, Mass. (1960). Includes quotes from Hardy, Fielding, Dickens, Zola, Trollope, Tolstoy and many others. Available second-hand via the internet.

William Archer, *Playmaking, A Manual of Craftmanship,* Chapman and Hall, London (1959) Dover Publications. Available second-hand via the internet.

William Ash, *The Way to Write Radio Drama,* Elm Tree Books, London; reissue (1985). Radio drama techniques including plot, theme, character and dialogue. Also covers what happens when a script is accepted for broadcast.

Donna Baker, *How to Write Stories for Magazines,* Allison and Busby, London; revised ed. (1995). Check with the library.

Michael Baldwin, *The Way to Write Poetry,* Elm Tree Books, London; reissue (1982). Check with the library.

H E.Bates, *The Modern Short Story*, Michael Joseph, London (1982) A critical survey of the short story. Available second-hand via the internet.

Carmel Bird, *Dear Writer,* Virago Press, London (1990). A classic guide to writing fiction. Available second-hand via the internet.

John Braine, *Writing a Novel,* Eyre Methuen, London (reissued as *How to Write a Novel*) Paperback. Methuen Publishing Ltd (1974). John Braine was both a novelist and book reviewer. This practical handbook is considered by many to be a classic guide to the art of writing a novel.

Dorothea Brande, *Becoming a Writer,* Macmillan, London; (new ed.) (1996) Pan – originally published in 1934. Writing techniques and exercises plus how to find the 'writer's magic'.

Brewer's Theatre, Cassell, Market House Books (1994). A phrase and fable dictionary devoted exclusively to the theatre.

Alison Chisholm, *The Craft of Writing Poetry,* Allison and Busby, London; 2nd ed. revised and updated (1998). A second revised and updated edition which provides basic and practical advice for aspiring poets, from first idea to final revision.

Brian Cooke, *Writing Comedy* for *Television,* Methuen, London (1983). Available second-hand via the internet.

Giles Cooper, *Radio Plays,* BBC Publications, London (1982). Distinguished plays from authors such as Jeremy Sandford. C. P. Taylor, Alan Sharpe. Available second-hand via the internet.

Christopher Derrick, *Reader's Report,* Victor Gollancz, London (May 1969). A publisher's reader gives the aspiring author advice on the pitfalls of submission. Available second-hand via the internet.

Jill Dick, *Freelance Writing for Newspapers,* A & C Black, London; 2nd ed. (1998). Brought up to date to include selling to internet publishers and covering topics from approaching a news editor to selling rights.

Jill Dick, *Writing for Magazines,* A & C Black, London; 2nd ed. (1996). Writing and selling non-fiction to magazines including interviewing and a section on electronic aids for the magazine writer.

Elizabeth Dipple, *Plot,* Methuen, London (1977). Available second-hand via the internet.

Jane Dorner, *The Internet: A Writer's Guide,* A & C Black, London; 2nd ed. (2001). A comprehensive guide for beginners and experts alike.

Jane Dorner, *Writing on Disk,* John Taylor Book Ventures, London (1992). Check with the library.

Dianne Doubtfire, *The Craft of Novel-Writing,* Allison and Busby, London, revised ed (1998).

John Fairfax and John Moat, *The Way to Write,* Penguin Books (1998). A practical guide for beginners which explains how to evaluate and improve your work.

Peter Finch, *How to Publish your Poetry,* Allison and Busby, London and New York; 4th ed. (1998). Essential topics for the would-be-published poet.

E. M. Forster, *Aspects of the Novel,* Penguin Books; new edition (2000). How to see through novels, not round them. A critical revision of the text by Oliver Stallybrass has given this much quoted title a new lease of life.

Pamela Frankau, *Pen to Paper,* William Heinemann, London (1961). A novelist's notebook. Available second-hand via the internet.

Natalie Goldberg, *Writing Down the Bones,* Shambhala Press, London (1993). Encouragement and advice on many aspects of the writer's craft from an off-beat and refreshing standpoint.

William Goldman, *Adventures in the Screen Trade,* Abacus, (1996). A personal yet practical view of screen writing.

Stuart Griffiths, *How Plays Are Made* Heinemann Educational, Secondary Division (1982). A guide to the basic principles of drama with a focus on structure.

John Herbert, *Radio Journalism,* A & C Black, London (1976). Gathering, editing and presenting material for broadcasting. Available second-hand via the internet

John Hines, *The Way to Write Non-Fiction,* Elm Tree Books, London (1990). Researching, writing and selling non-fiction books, market research, writing synopses, finding subject and publisher. Available second-hand via the internet.

Ann Hoffmann, *Research* for *Writers,* Writing Handbook London (1999) A research guide for writers and journalists offering practical advice on organization and methods of research.

Paddy Kitchen, *The Way to Write Novels,* Elm Tree Books, London; reissue (1981). A complete guide to the basic skills of good writing. Available second-hand via the internet.

Tessa Krailing, *How to Write for Children,* Allison and Busby, London (1996). How to find inspiration and get new ideas on writing for children of all age groups.

Barbara Kuroff (ed.) *Novel and Short Story Writer's Market,* Writer's Digest Books, F & W Publications, US (1999). A guide to US markets, publishers, agents, contests, conferences and awards.

Michael Legat, *The Writer's Rights,* Books for Writers, London (1995). A comprehensive guide to the legalities and business of being a published writer.

Michael Legat, *The Nuts and Bolts of Writing,* Robert Hale, London (1989). Available second-hand via the internet.

Michael Legat, *Writing* for *Pleasure and Profit,* Robert Hale, London (1993). Comprehensive guide for beginners.

Michael Legat, *Plotting the Novel,* Robert Hale, London (1992). Available second-hand via the internet.

Rhona Martin, *Writing Historical Fiction,* A & C Black, London; 2nd ed (1995). Different kinds of historical fiction are covered including: the family saga, the romance, the nostalgia novel, the adventure story, the 'straight' historical.

André Maurois, *The Art of Writing,* Bodley Head, London and Arno Press, New York (1960). European men of letters, including Voltaire, Tolstoy, Stendhal, Goethe and Flaubert. Available second-hand via the internet.

Kate Nivison, *How to Turn Your Holiday into Popular Fiction,* Allison and Busby, London (1994). Check with the library.

Eric Paice, *The Way to Write for Television,* Elm Tree Books, London; reissued rev. ed. (1987). A complete guide to the basic skills of writing television drama. Available second-hand via the internet.

J. B. Priestley, *The Art of the Dramatist,* William Heinemann Education, London (1973). The Inaugral Lecture, under the Hubert Henry Davies fund, given at the Old Vic Theatre on 30 September 1956 together with appendices and discursive notes. Available second-hand via the internet

B. A. Phythian, *Teach Yourself Correct English,* Hodder and Stoughton, London; 2nd ed. (2000). A practical guide and reference to improve the use of English in everyday life.

B. A. Phythian, *Teach Yourself English Grammar,* Hodder and Stoughton, London; revised ed. (1992). Chapters deal with the nature and function of all principle parts of speech and sentence structure. The exercises and tests provided reinforce learning.

John Ralph, *Teach Yourself the Internet for Writers*, Hodder and Stoughton, London (2000). A comprehensive guide to using the Web for success.

Ian Rodger, *Radio Drama,* Macmillan, London (1981). Available second-hand via the internet

Peter Sansom, *Writing Poems,* Bloodaxe Books, London (1994). Analysis, techniques and writing games, also metre rhyme, half-rhyme, free verse and given forms.

Jean Saunders, *The Craft of Writing Romance*, Writers' Bookshop (2000).

Jean Saunders, *Writing Step by Step.* Allison and Busby, London (1989). Check with the library.

William Smethhurst, *How to Write for Television,* How to Books, London (2000). Information and advice on all areas of writing for TV. Revised edition includes a rewritten chapter on opportunities for new writers plus a section on internet help sites and workshops.

Cathy Smith, *How to Write and Sell Travel Articles,* Allison and Busby, London (1992). Check with the library.

John Steinbeck, *Journal of a Novel,* Penguin Books (2001). A collection of letters forms a day-by-day account of Steinbeck's writing of *East of Eden,* his longest and most ambitious novel.

Frances Stillman, *The Poet's Manual,* Thames and Hudson, London (2000). A rhyming dictionary. This volume allows writers to find the rhymes they need easily.

William Strunk and E. B. White, *The Elements of Style,* 4th ed. hardback, Allyn and Bacon (1999). Offers advice on improving writing skills and promoting a style marked by simplicity, orderliness, and sincerity.

Ion Trewin, *Journalism,* David and Charles, London (1975). Available second-hand via the internet.

G. H. Vallins, *Good English,* Pan Books, London (1964). How to achieve a good, simple English style, whether for reports and stories or for business letters. Available second-hand via the internet.

G. H. Vallins, *Better English,* Pan Books, London (1955). Expands on the principles of clear writing and also deals with idiom, figure, the logical expressions of thought and the finer points of language. Available second-hand via the internet.

Gordon Wells, *The Craft of Writing Articles,* Allison and Busby, London; 2nd ed. (1996). A practical guide to writing feature articles and how to sell them.

Gordon Wells, *How to Write Non-Fiction Books*, Writers' Bookshop, London (1999). A step-by-step guide to writing and marketing a non-fiction book.

Gordon Wells, *The Magazine Writer's Handbook*, Allison and Busby, London (1985) and *The Magazine Writer's Handbook* (new edition) with Chris McCallum; Writers' Bookshop (2002) 8th ed. For all magazine writers – detailed information on many British magazines and comments on many more.

Gordon Wells, *Writers' Questions Answered*, Allison and Busby, London; Writers' Guides (2001). For beginners and the more experienced writers alike – provides useful information addressing many of the problems that can beset writers.

Stella Whitelaw, *How to Write and Sell a Book Proposal*, Writers' Bookshop, London (2000). An informative and entertaining guide to writing, writing synopses and proposals.

Mary Wibberley, *To Writers With Love*, Buchan and Enright, London (1993). A helpful guide to writing romance novels.

index

teach
yourself®

Afrikaans
Access 2002
Accounting, Basic
Alexander Technique
Algebra
Arabic
Arabic Script, Beginner's
Aromatherapy
Astronomy
Bach Flower Remedies
Bengali
Better Chess
Better Handwriting
Biology
Body Language
Book Keeping
Book Keeping & Accounting
Brazilian Portuguese
Bridge
Buddhism
Buddhism, 101 Key Ideas
Bulgarian
Business Studies
Business Studies, 101 Key Ideas
C++
Calculus
Calligraphy
Cantonese
Card Games
Catalan
Chemistry, 101 Key Ideas
Chess
Chi Kung
Chinese
Chinese, Beginner's
Chinese Language, Life & Culture
Chinese Script, Beginner's
Christianity
Classical Music

Copywriting
Counselling
Creative Writing
Crime Fiction
Croatian
Crystal Healing
Czech
Danish
Desktop Publishing
Digital Photography
Digital Video & PC Editing
Drawing
Dream Interpretation
Dutch
Dutch, Beginner's
Dutch Dictionary
Dutch Grammar
Eastern Philosophy
ECDL
E-Commerce
Economics, 101 Key Ideas
Electronics
English, American (EFL)
English as a Foreign Language
English, Correct
English Grammar
English Grammar (EFL)
English, Instant, for French Speakers
English, Instant, for German Speakers
English, Instant, for Italian Speakers
English, Instant, for Spanish Speakers
English for International Business
English Language, Life & Culture
English Verbs
English Vocabulary
Ethics
Excel 2002
Feng Shui
Film Making

Film Studies
Finance for non-Financial Managers
Finnish
Flexible Working
Flower Arranging
French
French, Beginner's
French Grammar
French Grammar, Quick Fix
French, Instant
French, Improve your
French Language, Life & Culture
French Starter Kit
French Verbs
French Vocabulary
Gaelic
Gaelic Dictionary
Gardening
Genetics
Geology
German
German, Beginner's
German Grammar
German Grammar, Quick Fix
German, Instant
German, Improve your
German Language, Life & Culture
German Verbs
German Vocabulary
Go
Golf
Greek
Greek, Ancient
Greek, Beginner's
Greek, Instant
Greek, New Testament
Greek Script, Beginner's
Guitar
Gulf Arabic
Hand Reflexology
Hebrew, Biblical
Herbal Medicine
Hieroglyphics
Hindi
Hindi, Beginner's
Hindi Script, Beginner's
Hinduism
History, 101 Key Ideas
How to Win at Horse Racing
How to Win at Poker
HTML Publishing on the WWW
Human Anatomy & Physiology
Hungarian
Icelandic
Indian Head Massage
Indonesian
Information Technology, 101 Key Ideas
Internet, The
Irish
Islam
Italian

Italian, Beginner's
Italian Grammar
Italian Grammar, Quick Fix
Italian, Instant
Italian, Improve your
Italian Language, Life & Culture
Italian Verbs
Italian Vocabulary
Japanese
Japanese, Beginner's
Japanese, Instant
Japanese Language, Life & Culture
Japanese Script, Beginner's
Java
Jewellery Making
Judaism
Korean
Latin
Latin American Spanish
Latin, Beginner's
Latin Dictionary
Latin Grammar
Letter Writing Skills
Linguistics
Linguistics, 101 Key Ideas
Literature, 101 Key Ideas
Mahjong
Managing Stress
Marketing
Massage
Mathematics
Mathematics, Basic
Media Studies
Meditation
Mosaics
Music Theory
Needlecraft
Negotiating
Nepali
Norwegian
Origami
Panjabi
Persian, Modern
Philosophy
Philosophy of Mind
Philosophy of Religion
Philosophy of Science
Philosophy, 101 Key Ideas
Photography
Photoshop
Physics
Piano
Planets
Planning Your Wedding
Polish
Politics
Portuguese
Portuguese, Beginner's
Portuguese Grammar
Portuguese, Instant
Portuguese Language, Life & Culture

Postmodernism
Pottery
Powerpoint 2002
Presenting for Professionals
Project Management
Psychology
Psychology, 101 Key Ideas
Psychology, Applied
Quark Xpress
Quilting
Recruitment
Reflexology
Reiki
Relaxation
Retaining Staff
Romanian
Russian
Russian, Beginner's
Russian Grammar
Russian, Instant
Russian Language, Life & Culture
Russian Script, Beginner's
Sanskrit
Screenwriting
Serbian
Setting up a Small Business
Shorthand, Pitman 2000
Sikhism
Spanish
Spanish, Beginner's
Spanish Grammar
Spanish Grammar, Quick Fix
Spanish, Instant
Spanish, Improve your
Spanish Language, Life & Culture
Spanish Starter Kit
Spanish Verbs
Spanish Vocabulary
Speaking on Special Occasions
Speed Reading
Statistical Research
Statistics
Swahili
Swahili Dictionary
Swedish
Tagalog
Tai Chi
Tantric Sex
Teaching English as a Foreign Language
Teaching English One to One
Teams and Team-Working
Thai
Time Management
Tracing your Family History
Travel Writing
Trigonometry
Turkish
Turkish, Beginner's
Typing
Ukrainian
Urdu

Urdu Script, Beginner's
Vietnamese
Volcanoes
Watercolour Painting
Weight Control through Diet and
  Exercise
Welsh
Welsh Dictionary
Welsh Language, Life & Culture
Wills and Probate
Wine Tasting
Winning at Job Interviews
Word 2002
World Faiths
Writing a Novel
Writing for Children
Writing Poetry
Xhosa
Yoga
Zen
Zulu

available from bookshops and on-line retailers